MW01169557

I Know A Woman…
Greenfire Wise Woman Craft

Pamela C. Kelly

Three Moons Media

Copyright ©2009 Pamela C. Kelly

All rights reserved. No part of this book may be reproduced or transmitted in any form or by any means, electronic or mechanical, including photocopying, recording or by any information storage and retrieval system, except for brief quotations within a review, without permission in writing from the author.

Published by Three Moons Media

1610 Valley Brook Lane

Longview, Texas 75605-2676

www.threemoonsmedia.com

Printed in the United States of America

ISBN 978-1-933514-12-3

Dedication and Thanks

To my husband for loving me through everything and for all his support.

To my mother for teaching me to write and for teaching me how to persevere.

To my father for asking me if I could paint that sunset
and for believing in fairies.

To my daughter for being my reason to continue this work.

To my son who taught me the meaning of heartbreak and forgiveness.

To Mark Lyons and Amy Krinner of Silver Broom Ministries
for giving me a home when I lost mine.

To Alice Agostini for putting me back together and
teaching me to say "I love you" again.

To Elder Cathryn "Darkstar" Byrnes for not allowing
me to quit in one of my darkest hours.

To Mommy Claudia for teaching me what it means to be a friend.

To Suzie for being a great neighbor and wonderful recipe "guinea pig."

To the Greenfire Clan's Melissa, its students, and
Reiki Practitioners—thank you.

To Marge Hartman for letting me borrow her book for two years—thank you!

To Grove Mother Lunaea Weatherstone and the Women of the Silver
Grove for setting wonderful examples of living an authentic life.

To the women of the Order of the White Moon—thank you.

To my teachers and role models—thank you for being so brave.

To our Foremothers before us and our children to come.

To the Divine for guidance, acceptance, strength, love and wisdom.

CONTENTS

THE CRONE

She came knocking at my door
That old hag—that whore
She came knocking at my door -
She said, "Dance with me some more"
She came knocking at my door
Wrinkled, frightening, yet someone I could adore
She came knocking at my door
"I have work, responsibilities," I implored
She came knocking at my door
"Daughter," she said, "your soul is poor"
She came knocking at my door
Angrily I said, "You I will ignore!"
She came knocking at my door
"Then sickness you will endure"
She came knocking at my door
Gnarled hands beckoning she lured
She came knocking at my door
"Be gentle, I'm worn!"
She came knocking at my door
"It's time to be reborn!"
She came knocking at my door
Through me her eyes bored
She came knocking at my door
"Into my cauldron!" she roared
She came knocking at my door
For my soul to dance, to change, to soar
Now I come knocking at your door…

—Pamela C. Kelly, January 2009

CHAPTER 1

HERSTORY OF GREENFIRE WISE WOMAN CRAFT

Aengus is a deathless comrade of the Spring, and we may well pray to him to let
his green fire move in our veins.

—Fiona MacLeod, *The Birds of Aengus Og*,
in *The Celtic Spirit*. Matthews, 1999.

Greenfire Wise Woman Craft is so called because the word "witchcraft" is too emotion-ally charged. It is also limiting in its sphere of influence because witchcraft would only reach out to pagans and not help those who wish to remain in their religions. Marion Green explains it this way, "Real witches do not, and never have, called themselves 'witches'; that is a term applied by others. They might say they are interested in the Old Ways...Some are members of orthodox faiths as well." (Green, 1991.) Wise Woman Craft refers to all women in the process of relearning and remembering their grandmothers' wisdom. Kiva Rose describes her role: "The path of the Medicine Woman lies outside the walls of religious dictates. It often survives as a subversive current within the shadow of existing beliefs. These women live on the fringes of their people—always needed but rarely accepted. The same woman who is called a bruja or witch in times of health may be respectfully approached as a healer during times of crisis." (Rose, 2008.)

Throughout herstory there have been many wise women. Often we do not have a written record of these women. This is due to the oral traditions of a mostly illiterate people who taught this wisdom quietly in their kitchens and their gardens. When we look back into our own family herstories we find them in the leaves, roots and branches of our own clan's trees.

They are the women who whispered in our ears the secret ingredient for a recipe, when to plant, when to weed, or harvest. It doesn't matter what our religion is or what theirs was, the wisdom is woven in every family's tapestries. In some cultures they spit or blew on us to protect us from evil or gave us a new broom when we moved to a new home because it is bad luck to bring the broom from the old house. We learned various traditions and types of healings from a time when a doctor was not available or affordable. As we collect these stories like tattered cloth from an old quilt, we re-attach all the little pieces to help us remember our legacy.

There are some legends that survived, such as Biddy Early, an Irish wise woman who performed divination using a blue bottle. Then there was Meg the Healer who was permitted to walk freely between our world and the fairy world because she was such a wonderful healer. (McCoy, 1998.) We read about theories of Avalon where women learned the arts of herbal lore and healing. In the Old Testament we learn about Shiphrah and Puah who were the Jewish midwives commanded by Pharaoh to kill all male babies born. They did not, saying the Jewish women were too strong and the babies were born before they arrived. With their courage and knowledge the children of the Jews were allowed to live. (Exodus 1:15–22.) St. Hildegard of Bingen, Germany, was an eleventh-century herbalist, abbess, composer, and mystic. She used the word "viriditas," which is translated as the greening power, to describe the healing power of the Earth and her plants. (Berger, 1998.) Our foremothers who came to the United States preferred the midwife to the male American doctor, saying that she was more affordable, took care of the other children, prepared a meal and lit a fire before she left. The women also found that they and their babies had a better survival rate with a midwife because, unlike the male doctor, she knew to wash her hands before touching the expectant mother, and she did not rush the mother's delivery with forceps, but allowed the mother to bring the child into the world in her own time. (Weatherford, 1995.)

W. R. Wallace said, "For the hand that rocks the cradle is the hand that rules the world." When we take this into consideration as we take on the roles of aunt, mother, big sister, grandmother, or friend, we are the first teachers for our children. So as wise women re-weaving our ancestor's wisdom, we have the ability to change the world one child at a time while we rock their cradles.

This art can also be called a folk craft because it is a series of skills done by the common woman in her home, garden or kitchen. There are no special tools, clothes or symbols for us because we incorporate the Divine into the mundane every day. Many of us continue to attend church, synagogue, ashram or coven. Some of us find this path to be our religion by honoring the seasons, the phases of the moon, by growing our medicines and making them into tinctures, tea or cream.

When I started studying the green path, I had also started learning Reiki. As I continued my studies I incorporated my training in crystal and chakra therapies as well as aromatherapy. What I found was that they overlapped and complemented each other. I originally began this course of study when I was pregnant. Then I had a miscarriage. The doctor had a look at me and sent me home. I started to take and grow herbs to heal myself. I did my first ritual to heal over my loss. What happened to me at that point was life-changing. Something inside me cracked open. I held myself together during the day to howl uncontrollably like a wolf in the shower out of sorrow every night. I howled from deep inside of me, in a place I did not know existed. Something, or should I say someone, came out—it was my wild woman.

Clarissa Pinkola Estes says in *Women Who Run with the Wolves: Myths and Stories of the Wild Woman Archetype*, "So like many women before and after me, I lived my life as a disguised *creatura*, creature. Like my kith and kin before me, I swaggered-staggered in high heels, and I wore a dress and hat to church. But my fabulous tail often fell below my hemline, and my ears twitched until my hat pitched, at the very least down over both my eyes, and sometimes clear across the room. I've not forgotten the song of those dark years, *hambre del alma*, the song of the starved soul. But neither have I forgotten the joyous *canto hondo*, the deep song, the words of which come back to us when we do the work of soulful reclamation." (Estes, 1992.)

Z. Budapest tells us that we need to reach out to our inner wild woman and suggests we meditate to meet her. She tells us to honor her by going outside, exercising and eating fresh fruit or vegetables. (Budapest, 1993.) When we do this we are more balanced and grounded. That is the goal for each Greenfire Wise Woman: to be more grounded, connected to her own inner knowing, her wild woman. After a traditional thirteen moons of study they are herbalists, trained in the Wise Woman tradition, Reiki masters, aromatherapy, crystal and chakra therapists. They have worked with an herbal ally growing, sitting with, singing to, harvesting, tincturing, making infusions, oils and salves of it. The year is demanding, and with the soul-searching some women take more than a year. Others quit and never return because they do not want to make the changes this path demands. However, those who complete the work are forever changed.

Notes—Herstory of Greenfire Wise Woman Craft

Berger, J. *Herbal Rituals.* New York: St. Martin's Press, 1998.

Budapest, Z. *The Goddess in the Office: A Personal Energy Guide for the Spiritual Warrior at Work.* New York: HarperCollins Publishers, 1993.

Estes, C. *Women Who Run With the Wolves: Myths and Stories of the Wild Woman Archetype.* New York: Ballantine Books, 1992.

Green, M. *A Witch Alone.* London: Thorsons, 1991.

Kelly, P. *The Crone.* Oakdale: Greenfire Wise Woman Craft, 2009.

Holy Bible Revised Standard Version. Book of Exodus. Chicago: International Council of Religious Education, 1928.

McCoy, E. *Celtic Women's Spirituality: Accessing the Cauldron of Life.* St. Paul: Llewellyn Publications, 1998.

Matthews, C. *The Celtic Spirit.* New York: HarperCollins Publishers, 1999.

Rose, K. "The Wild Maiden." *Sage Woman—Celebrating the Goddess in Every Woman, Issue 74, 33–36, 2008.*

Wallace, W. *Magill's Quotations in Context.* New York: Harper & Row, 1896.

Weatherford, D. *Foreign and Female: Immigrant Women in America, 1840–1930.* New York: Facts on File, Inc, 1995.

CHAPTER 2

REIKI I

I believe there exists One Supreme Being—the Absolute Infinite—a Dynamic
Force that governs the world and universe. It is an unseen spiritual power that
vibrates and all other powers fade into insignificance beside it. So, therefore, it is
Absolute!...I shall call it "Reiki."...Being a universal force from the Great Divine
Spirit, it belongs to all who seek and desire to learn the art of healing.
> —Hawayo Takata in *Essential Reiki*, Stein, 1996.

THE FINE PRINT

Reiki is an Asian system of healing that heals body, mind, emotions and spirit. The concept behind the program is similar to the thinking we see in Indian, Chinese and Japanese types of healing. If there is something wrong or damaged with the emotions or spirit, it will affect the body.
Reiki, like Wise Woman Craft, is a holistic approach to healing and, unlike traditional types of
Western healing, which views the person as a machine with parts, Reiki addresses all aspects of
the person. When people study Reiki they are often beginning a journey for personal healing. If
a person does not come to Reiki to heal first, but to study to become a healer, they will find that
there is work to be done within themselves prior to being qualified to treat others.

Sometimes people come to Reiki because they have exhausted all other methods. What they
do not realize is that looks can be deceiving. When a person goes for a Reiki treatment there
is often incense and New Age music. Perhaps there are flowers and low lights or aromatherapy
treatments. People think, "Oh, this is going to be easy," because there are no fluorescent lights,

"stiff-lipped, white coats" who make you wait 1½ hours for a 10-minute appointment only to hurt you with some procedure or test. What they do not realize is that the issues that brought about their illness will come up during treatment, and they will need to face those issues in order to continue on with the healing process. It should be noted that sometimes people just get sick. We cannot figure out why; it is not due to sin or wrongdoing. In a situation like that, the emotions that will come up will be about dealing with the illness. The other approach is to utilize the treatments alongside modern medicine. This type of thinking has started to reach the mainstream population and now nurses are getting CEUs in the study of Reiki. No matter what path a person takes, if they decide to incorporate this alternative healing treatment into their life, they will need to face their inner demons and scars from the past.

But the reality is no matter what your reason for coming to Reiki things are going to come up—sometimes literally. Years ago I had a friend who had been repeatedly sexually abused as a child. When she was older, married with two children, she reached a very pressured time in her life. She gained a lot of weight and started to have panic attacks. My friend went into therapy and for a long time she held the wastepaper basket, throwing up throughout each session. Her therapist said she could no longer bury the pain, and so it is with Reiki. Where you may not receive a physical shot or surgery, you will receive an emotional or spiritual one. Things you thought were over come up to rear their ugly heads. What does this mean for the recipient of Reiki? You still need to do "the work": journaling, meditation, prayer, affirmations, forgiveness, and when necessary, therapy. There is no shortcut. Reiki accelerates your development and there is no turning back.

From an Eastern paradigm, this means if one has a broken heart that has not healed it will be manifested as heart trouble. Perhaps one has not forgiven someone or still has a tremendous amount of anger. Then a person shouldn't be surprised that this might manifest as liver trouble. In Chinese medicine anger resides in the liver. Fear manifests in the kidneys. So when one comes to a Reiki treatment for a restful, healing treatment, understand that the issues that may have brought on the physical ailment will come up to be addressed. Therefore it should be noted that there are times when people feel ill at ease after a treatment. There can be sadness or introspection, whereupon issues once buried resurface and now must be released once and for all. That is why I often ask people who come for a treatment if they have a therapist they go to when they need to, and if they do not, I will recommend one should they feel they need to work through an issue.

It is believed among many Reiki practitioners that those who come to get Reiki training had Reiki in a previous life. If one is working with a person who does not believe in past lives, then we can say it is in their gene memory from their ancestors. In Wise Woman Craft there should be no dogma, but a willingness to work within someone's belief systems, with a little tug on either side of their brain and soul to stretch their existing paradigm.

To utilize Reiki one must believe in a higher power. Students must remember that they are not doing the healing, but they are merely a conduit for the Divine to come and heal. Therefore, when someone comes to me for an attunement I specifically ask what they believe in, who they worship, if anyone, what their spiritual beliefs and practices are. Sometimes people are taken aback; they think I am being nosey. When I explain to them that this is not faith healing based on their faith and willingness to repent their sins, but a system based on energy, it makes more sense to them. Christians look at this as God is in everything and everyone, similar to the Sunday School song, "This Little Light of Mine." If a person does not believe in a specific deity but the Universal Life Force, that's fine because we can move energy to where it needs to go for a healing.

Reiki heals the healer as well as the healee. If we view ourselves as a conduit, it makes sense, because we are like an electrical cord where energy goes through us and out of us to heal others. This Divine energy touches us as it passes, so it will heal us too.

We never really know the outcome, the Divine's plan or the Universal plan for ourselves or someone else. We can speak of our impressions, things we "see" or "feel" as we do a healing, but we do not know God's plan. At this point I would like to note that the word "God" once referred to both the Divine feminine and masculine energy. It is only since patriarchal thinking invaded our thought processes that we are so specific. Julia Cameron, author of *The Artist's Way: A Spiritual Path to Higher Creativity*, discusses her use of the word God, "...in essence, a spiritual path, initiated and practiced through creativity, this book uses the word 'God.' This may be volatile to some of you...Please be open-minded." (Cameron, 1992.) And so when we approach the healing of another or ourselves, we do not know what God wants for us. It could mean helping someone with unfinished business before they cross over, giving them a peaceful death. There are many factors in why someone doesn't heal, and we are not responsible for that. We come to the Divine's table offering ourselves up to heal and be healed, asking that we do our best. We cannot control what the client will do, whether or not they change their lifestyle to be at peace; we can only control ourselves. Remember the Christian saying, "Do your best and let God do the rest."

Reiki history

Dr. Usui is considered to be the founder of Reiki. There are different stories about him. Some say he was a Presbyterian minister, others say this was said to make Reiki more acceptable to Westerners. Still other sources say Reiki is an ancient form of Tibetan healing. Whatever the real story is, many feel Reiki works and makes a difference in their lives.

While I am a lineaged Usui Reiki master and teacher, and I train my students in the traditional teachings, I branch off to have them study from Diane Stein's book, *Essential Reiki: A Complete Guide to an Ancient Healing Art.* Diane is a Goddess-loving woman, so I forewarn my traditional Judeo-Christian students of this. However, I have never found a more comprehensive source. Diane received tremendous criticism from the Reiki community for her work because she published all the secret Reiki symbols and she is very eclectic in her approach. Last I read, I do not believe Diane had her Reiki/Master/Teacher certificates, yet she gave attunements and taught others. This outraged the traditional Usui community. To add to this criticism, Diane included non-traditional symbols, their use and meanings in her book, which would never have been taught from a traditional Usui master. Not only does her book include the hand positions and the symbols, as well as how to give an attunement, she also includes how to do a group healing.

When Mrs. Takamato brought Reiki to the United States after being cured of terminal cancer in a traditional Reiki clinic, she believed Americans did not appreciate anything that wasn't expensive so she charged $10,000 for an attunement. (Stein, 1996.) The traditional Reiki community was in support of this philosophy and charged large amounts of money for each attunement level and kept the symbols a secret. When a person gets their Level I Reiki attunement from a traditional Usui teacher, they are not shown the symbols or explained their meaning. These symbols are placed permanently in a person. One of my students traveled to California from New York to study with such a teacher. She went to an extensive weekend workshop training to receive all the levels. She was told what her prayer of intention should be; she was not permitted to receive printed symbols or write the symbols. She paid thousands of dollars and came to study with me because she never felt the Reiki "took." She didn't connect with the prayer of intention she was told to memorize, either. When I teach Reiki I, I show people what the symbols look like and explain their meaning. These symbols will be implanted permanently in the person's aura, therefore I believe they should know what is happening. When I teach the prayer of intention, I ask my students to develop one on their own, as my teachers did. This makes the process more personal and meaningful for the student.

My teachers and Diane Stein believe that in order to change the world we must make Reiki more accessible. It should be more readily available for treatments as well as trainings. Diane felt that Usui Reiki was becoming an elitist art and not serving humankind as it should. Imagine what the world would be like if every mother and father, every caregiver had at least Reiki I to heal themselves and those they cared for? What would life be like for us?

REIKI PRINCIPLES

There are several versions of the Reiki principles; they all express the same values. Here is the version I learned from my teacher:

> *Just for today do not worry.*
> *Just for today do not anger.*
> *Honor your parents, teachers, and elders.*
> *Earn your living honestly.*
> *Show gratitude to everything.*

These principles were said to have been given by the Reiki founder, Mikao Usui. It should be given to students as soon as they start studying Reiki I. This gives them a focus and guideline to return to. (Stein, 1996.)

GIVING ATTUNEMENTS AND HEALINGS

In Greenfire Wise Woman Craft we try to make Reiki as available for treatment or training as possible. Some of us volunteer for hospice, we barter for attunements if money is not available, and sometimes we give Reiki I for free to the seriously ill so they can heal themselves or ease their pain. This is done with the hope that we are slowly, in our own way, making a difference in the world.

Before I do an attunement or a healing I tell the person where my hands will go. I do not have to touch the person to give an attunement or healing. Sometimes people have been hurt and I do not know about it. I want the person receiving Reiki to feel safe. At no time does a person need to undress or be touched in a personal way or area. If a person goes for a massage and then Reiki that might be the only time when a person might be undressed, but even then they should be covered with a sheet. I want my Reiki recipients to feel safe so they can benefit fully from the session.

At the beginning of an attunement or healing I cleanse myself, the person, and the space. This can be done with smudge or envisioning the person, ourselves and the space in white light. I can then make sacred space; this can be as simple or elaborate as I want. If I am in a hospital room for instance, putting the Reiki Symbols around me and the person being treated works well. Some people call the angels while others light incense and candles, putting crystals around with peaceful music playing. It is really according to your tastes, the situation and the needs of your client. If someone has terrible allergies, candles and incense would not be appreciated. I always ask if someone has allergies before I smudge the room. That is why it is important to know other ways to clear a room and make sacred space without scent or smoke.

After I clear and make sacred space, I say my prayer of intention. This is a request to the Universe, your Deity, Saint of choice, or guides for permission to do Reiki, give an attunement or healing, as well as for protection and guidance. Some people stand in Wu Chi (nothingness stance from Tai Chi) and do the micro-cosmic orbit prior to a Reiki Session. [Illustration at right] Some people were trained to ask the person permission to heal or attune them after this. I usually do not do this because the person would not be there if they didn't want the Reiki. It seems something of a moot point.

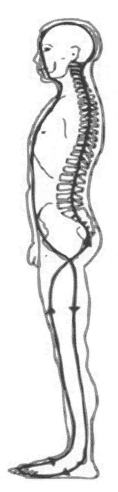

It is important for the Reiki practioner giving an attunement or doing the micro-cosmic orbit to contract their Hui Yin. The Hui Yin is in the perineum area between the genitals and the anus. This is the same as doing a Kegel exercise that women are recommended to do after childbirth and during menopause. The only difference is that you are not releasing the muscles but holding them. While doing this, the tongue should be pressed to the roof of the mouth. By doing this, the practitioner holds the Ki in and makes it circulate within the body. Diane Stein points out that the Hui Yin position is the major difference between nontraditional and traditional Reiki. Traditional initiations have four attunements in the First degree and one in the Second. When one uses the Hui Yin contraction, the Hara Line is activated making only one attunement necessary for each degree. The Hara is located in the belly between the navel and the Belly chakra. In India it is called the Sacral Center and in China it is called the Triple Warmer. In Japan they teach that a central channel comes from this area and travels up through the chakras and the etheric double. Reiki III involves a single attunement for both traditional and nontraditional methods. (Stein, 1996.)

There are three symbols that are used in an attunement for Reiki I and II (see chart below). Cho-Ku-Rei loosely means put the energy here or God is here. This symbol heals the physical body. Sei-He-Ki, the second symbol, has different translations: God and man coming together, or As Above, So Below. It is for emotional healing, purification, protection, and clearing. Hon-She-Ze-Sho-Nen, the third symbol, is for distance healing, the Akashic Records, or the past, present and future. This symbol heals the mental body. It has also been said that it will clear away Karma. (Stein, 1996.)

Reiki Symbol	Meaning
	Cho—Full Ku—Ceremonial vessel Rei—Transcended mystery, holy spirit or universal life force Fill this with the creative or holy spirit; also means put the power here.
	Sei—Well-being He—Creator Ki—Personal life force, man and God uniting or man and God becoming one. For emotional healing.
	Hon—Origin Sha—Person Ze—Through a tunnel of Light to a higher dimension Sho—Real Nen—Prayer, psychic power and meditation. The Divine in me reaches out to the Divine in you. It creates a bridge beyond time and space.

Reiki Symbol	Meaning
	DaiKoMyo—Great bright light. Ultimate healing symbol. Traditional version.
	DaiKoMyo—Great bright light. Ultimate healing symbol. Non-traditional version.
	Raku—Used for passing attunements and grounding energy at the end of the attunement.

The traditional places to put the symbols on the person are the head and hands. I start by going in front of the person and opening their aura, starting at their crown and bringing my hands down on either side of them to their feet. Then I ask that they put their hands together in prayer pose, and I stand behind them. The three symbols that go into the crown chakra are the Cho-Ku-Rei, Sei-He-Ki and the Hon-She-Ze-Sho-Nen. One of my teachers believed that after placing the symbols or completing a treatment the chakra should be sealed with a Cho-

Ku-Rei. Then the Reiki practitioner should walk around the front of the person, and taking a hand, write the symbol Cho-Ku-Rei in it and gently slap or press the symbol in. I had one teacher who wrote the symbol in the hand three times and another who wrote it once. After the symbol is pressed into the hand, the hand is laid across the person's chest and the process is repeated for the other hand. Then their arms should be crossed over their chest. I wait for a moment allowing them to absorb and enjoy the energy of the symbol. This is repeated for Sei-He-Kei and Hon-She-Zhe-Sho-Nen.

At this point most teachers will walk behind the client to then proceed to the next step. When I started to give attunements, I felt that symbols should also be placed in each chakra. I cup my hands over each chakra and place the three symbols in it. I also place the symbols in the chakras in the knees and feet as they are important minor chakras. This is what I teach my students. I suggest that they do it, but it is not required, nor is it considered a traditional Reiki attunement procedure.

I then walk around the client, holding my Hui Yin, and reach in front of them bringing their prayer hands up. Separating their hands in a cup, I blow each symbol into the crown and hands. Then I place their hands in prayer pose, in front of their heart chakra. Walking in front of the student, I reach down at the person's feet and bring the aura back up, leaving it open at the crown chakra to keep the client connected to the Divine.

Most practitioners usually brush an aura after a treatment or attunement. Some people smudge around the person, others sweep the person with their hands or a crystal. Kyanite is especially useful for this as it seals up the holes in an aura and rarely, if ever, needs to be cleansed. If a person has been trained in an American Indian tradition, they might use feathers to brush the aura. Ting-shas (cymbals) are nice to use, letting the person know the session is over, bringing them out of a deep meditative state, as well as cleansing and sealing the aura.

Many times after a session has ended, a person will open up and tell the healer their impressions, and the physical and emotional pains experienced. They might be amazed and spacey, too. Anything shared in a session should be kept in strictest of confidence.

When people receive an attunement they might feel different for a few days afterward. They may be sleepy or energized, women might get their period, and a person might experience diarrhea or frequent urination with dark urine. They may feel moody or introspective. The measure of whether or not it is an illness is whether they feel ill.

Hand positions for self-healing

For the next 21 days after a Reiki I attunement the person should Reiki themselves every day using the positions listed below.

Front of the body

- Eyes/third eye
- Temples/ears
- Back of the head
- The throat
- T on the heart
- Lower ribs
- Above the navel/below the navel
- Pelvic bones
- Pubic bones
- Knees
- Ankles and bottom of feet

Back of the body

- Behind the top of the head and behind the head
- Back of neck
- Shoulders—Use this area to send Reiki through the body to the feet.
- Middle back
- Lower back over sacrum
- Back of knees
- Ankles and feet

Hand positions for healing others

Front of the body

- Hands cupped over eyes
- Temples/ears
- Hand under head

- Collarbone just below throat
- Over heart—Respect your client's privacy: do not touch breasts.
- Below breasts over lower ribs
- Lower navel
- Over pelvic area above pubic bone
- Over pubic bone—Do not touch groin area: cup your hands above the area.
- Front of knees
- Front of ankles
- Bottoms of feet

BACK OF THE BODY

- Back of neck
- Over shoulder blades
- Middle of back
- Lower back over sacrum
- Over tailbone/coccyx
- Backs of knees
- Backs of ankles
- Bottoms of feet

My teachers always said that the energy was for just the client in the beginning. It is safe to Reiki your plants and animals, your food, drinks, herbs and medicine. Remember that when a person does Reiki on their medicine, they should pay attention to how they feel. Many people find they need to reduce their dosages when they do this.

Keeping the energy for you is not necessarily the same philosophy as other teachers. If you take a crash course for all three levels you will never have 21 days to absorb the energy and feel the changes. Diane Stein and other teachers feel there is no problem with new Reiki I students healing other people. I found the energy flow that I was suddenly opened up to very disconcerting, and it took me a while to get used to the energy. Diane believed the Reiki protected you and it would be fine. I find that my students, like me, are psychics and empaths already. We tend to absorb people's energy. We know who is calling on the phone, what people are thinking, synchronicity rules our lives. Many students may not know why and simply call it a coincidence. They may not know what synchronicity is or how it works. It is for this reason that I follow my teachers' advice and wait between levels of attunement. Reiki opens your interconnectedness to the Universe; there will be changes in your perception. I remember when I first started practicing Reiki and I went to heal a birch on our property. I stood in Wu Chi, said my prayers with my hands in prayer pose, and put my hands on her. The tree said, "I am dying." Now, I did not hear it with my physical ear but my "inner ear." The next season, the tree died. Unfortunately, my teachers did not warn me that things like this would happen. When I went back to them they confirmed that this is common. I would have preferred that they had told me ahead of time.

Aura cleansing and protection

Some say that people who get Reiki are already vibrating at a higher level before they receive the attunement. After the attunement they vibrate at an even higher level. It is for this reason I teach my students to protect their energy at the end of the Reiki I class. When I received my Reiki I, I was too open and everyone took my energy, both people at work and home. I went back to my teacher for a treatment, and she said I was depleted. She told me I should have protected myself; honestly, I wish she had told me before I left after my attunement. It is for this reason I go over with my students, and expect them to teach their students, the need for protection and recharging. I call recharging "re-filling your well."

Now, this is not a section to make you paranoid, but let's face it, we *all* have a psychic vampire in our lives. Some of us have more than one; you know the one at work, home, in the neighborhood, or extended family that comes with a big straw to suck the life out of you until you're dry. They walk in a room and it's like a great black hole has entered. Similar to the dementors in the Harry Potter books, all the joy is sucked out of the room. It must be noted that 90 percent of these people do not consciously do this; they have no real plan to take your energy, but they do. Sometimes they are going through a divorce or loss, other times they are just miserable, needy people who will never get their act together.

As I said it doesn't mean these people are evil, nor are they intentionally drawing all your energy, but they are not allowed to do that. This means that when a Reiki practitioner gets up in the morning they put a protection around themselves. There are many ways to do this; the first method I use is what I call the "Psychic Blankie." The person pictures a white blanket, similar to the old fashioned Halloween ghost costume over them. The protection goes all the way to the ground where it remains open around their feet. This way any negativity within the person is recycled back into the Earth. In Tai Chi, I was taught to put my white net around me which comes from my Tan Tien, the center of my being, in the area of the sacral chakra. Some people just put white light around themselves. Whatever it is, do it every day before you leave the house and whenever you run into your vampire. Sometimes the light will come out another color. My view on this has always been to go with it, it is the color the Universe or your Deity is giving you to protect you today. Smudging yourself, using tingshas (chimes) over your aura or brushing it with a piece of kyanite are other ways to clear negativity.

Even with our protections, there are days when we are depleted and need to refill our well. In her book *Jambalaya*, Luiseh Tesh explains a West African aura cleansing. She rinses her hands and brushes each section of the aura (front, back, sides and head), periodically rinsing off her hands; she continually does this until her aura is clean. This means a person may need to go back over the aura. Although Luiseh does this even in a restroom, I find I get myself and the floor wet. When I do it on another person I do not think they are appreciative of the dripping water, and it takes away from the relaxed atmosphere. I recommend to my students to do this in the shower. Since most of my students are women it is safe to assume the shower is a place where they (hopefully) will not be interrupted. (Teish, 1985.) Some of the Greenfire women are counselors, massage therapists or tattoo artists. For them I stress protecting and cleansing themselves between clients so their energy will not drain away.

Silver Ravenwolf uses an auric visualization technique that is called "Liquid Light." "Sit in a quiet place where you will be undisturbed for at least five minutes. Take three deep breaths and exhale slowly. Close your eyes. Envision white light encompassing your auric body. Imagine that the light coalesces into a glittering, sacred liquid of spiritual, mental and physical transformation. Allow this liquid light to pour into your auric field from all edges of the auric body. The path of the light slowly flows into your heart chakra from all directions until you are totally filled with pure white light energy. Continue until no speck of darkness remains and you feel your inner self vibrating with pure potential and power. Take three deep breaths and open your eyes. The exercise is completed. If you like, begin and end the session with the sound of a bell or chimes." (Ravenwolf, 2005.)

Communing with nature, hugging trees, sitting on the ground, caring for your garden are all ways to clear yourself of negativity and ground your energy. These activities are especially helpful after giving or receiving Reiki. I used to have terrible PMS when I started down this path. My Reiki teacher told me to weed my garden when I felt like this to ground my energy. I have always found this helpful even when I am nervous or upset.

Notes—Reiki I

Cameron, J. *The Artist's Way: A Spiritual Path to Higher Creativity.* New York: Putnam Books, 1992.

Ravenwolf, S. *A Witch's Notebook.* St. Paul: Llewellyn Publications, 2005.

Reiki For Holistic Health. Retrieved January 18, 2009 from www.reiki-for-holistic-health.com/reiki-hand-positions.html, 2003.

Stein, D. *Essential Reiki.* Freedom: The Crossing Press, Inc., 1996.

Teish, L. *Jambalaya: The Natural Woman's Book of Personal Charms and Practical Rituals.* San Francisco: Harper, 1985.

CHAPTER 3

REIKI II & III

Mother of our mothers, Foremothers strong,
Guide our hands in yours, Remind us how to kindle the hearth.
　　　　　—Caitlin Matthews, *A Blessing for the Hearth Keepers*, 1999.

The attunement for Reiki II is the same as Reiki I except that the practitioner asks permission to give a Level II attunement. At this level the student must know the symbols by memory. I had to draw them on my teacher's back when I was learning because I was not permitted to write them on paper. This is the level where a student can do a distance healing using the symbol Hon-She-Zhe-Sho-Nen. Some people can just picture the person and it works for them. Others need a picture or toy. Write the name of the person needing the healing on a piece of paper. When my father had a stroke, I wrote his name on a piece of paper and put it in my trouser pocket. Throughout the day I would take it out and send Reiki to him.

At this level people are more comfortable with Reiki and have started to give treatments to friends and family. I always encourage people to participate in Reiki circles to give as well as receive Reiki. We practice on each other during class and sometimes students bring friends who need healing.

Reiki II stresses the meaning of the symbols. I ask my students to meditate on each one individually over a period of time. They should know what each symbol feels like and what it can do. This will also make them surer of themselves as they work on others.

REIKI III

So often it seems that many Reiki Masters and practitioners are overly sensitive to things like lineage, certificates, and membership in the "right" organization. The important thing is: Do you know within yourself that you are connected to Reiki? If you do, then nothing else matters.

—Ms. Furumoto, Mrs. Takata's granddaughter and Grand Master of the Reiki Alliance, in Diane Stein, *Essential Reiki*, 1996.

Third degree Reiki is the teaching degree where a student can pass on Reiki to others. Some traditional Reiki Masters make the third degree and teaching degree separate. Other truly traditional teachers require that a student pay exorbitant amounts of money to apprentice with them and after a period of a year or more, at the teacher's discretion, the student may receive their level III. The student is not permitted to ask for the attunement. (Stein, 1996.)

There are two symbols used for attunement of the third degree. The first is Dai-Ko-Myo. This is the symbol used for healings and for transmitting Reiki Attunements. There are several versions of the traditional symbol shown in the chart. The non-traditional Dai-Ko-Myo has more of a feminine energy. I often find that I use the traditional Dai-Ko-Myo on men, which is more linear, and the non-traditional on women, the spiral energy. There have been times when I used the non-traditional symbol on a man and it was for healing his issues with women, specifically his mother. Diane Stein has used this symbol to clear, charge, and program crystals, as well as to ask them to become self-clearing.

The last symbol used for the level III is the Raku which is the lightning bolt and is only used for passing attunements. It is drawn down the back of a person at the end of the attunement to ground the energy. It activates the Hara Line and grounds it in the navel.

At this level a person must have all the five symbols memorized. They must practice holding in their Hui Yin to give an attunement. When I teach I have the students practice on each other so they will be comfortable and confident. Prior to Reiki III, I ask students to sit and meditate with each symbol so they know its energy intimately. I teach Master and teacher together because that is how I was taught, and I cannot justify charging someone more money to receive an additional level. The students work on ethics, group healings, and practicing giving attunements so students leave with a broad base of knowledge.

The attunement is what makes Reiki different from other energy or touch healing systems.

Diane Stein explains attunements in her book *Essential Reiki: A Complete Guide to an Ancient Healing Art,* "Reiki attunements open and expand the Ki-holding capacity of the Hara Line and clear the channels of energy blockage. They clear and balance the Hara Line chakras and the chakras' etheric double. During an attunement, Heavenly Ki energy carrying the five Reiki symbols moves from the Crown to the receiver's Heart. Earthly Ki is drawn through the legs and lower centers from the Hara to the Heart as well. Original Ki in the Hara center is replenished and refilled, and any obstructions to the energy's full use are removed. All this happens in a matter of something less than a few minutes." (Stein, 1996.)

Notes—Reiki II & III

Matthews, C. *The Celtic Spirit.* New York: HarperCollins Publishers, 1999.

Reiki Living. Retrieved January 18, 2009 from www.reikiliving.com/Reiki%20Symbols.htm, 2003.

Stein, D. *Essential Reiki.* Freedom: The Crossing Press, Inc., 1996.

Teish, L. *Jambalaya The Natural Woman's Book of Personal Charms and Practical Rituals.* New York: Harper Collins Publishers, 1985.

CHAPTER 4

Chakra Therapy

> Do not cringe and make yourself small if you are called the black sheep, the maverick, the lone wolf. Those with slow seeing say a nonconformist is a blight on society. But it has been proven over the centuries, that being different means standing at the edge, means one is practically guaranteed to make an original contribution, a useful and stunning contribution to her culture.
> — Clarissa Pinkola Estes, *Women Who Run With the Wolves*, 1992.

Chakra, in Sanskrit, means wheel and we adjust this wheel to move faster or slower. Each major chakra has a color associated with it. When the chakra is adjusted it affects the corresponding color in the aura. In Indian Ayurvedic medicine it is believed that every chakra in the energy body affects a part of the physical body. By cleansing and adjusting the chakras the body is able to heal. Chakras also affect the spiritual and emotional aspects of a person's life. Therefore if you adjust the chakras issues, fears, anger or other emotions may rise to the top to be released in order to let the person heal.

There are different techniques taught to cleanse and adjust a chakra. I have read that traditional Indian Ayurvedic teachers will often tell a person that it is extremely dangerous to adjust chakras. Yet there are many teachers, including Reiki practitioners and crystal therapists, that will teach how to work with them. The Wise Woman method encourages tapping into your inner cauldron of wisdom, knowledge and intuition to heal yourself and others. Therefore adjusting your own chakras or a client's is part of the treatment. Diane Stein recommends putting the corresponding crystal on the person's chakra to adjust it and when the stone falls off the chakra is done. (Stein, 2000.) The use of colored squares of cloth or paper has been incorporated by some to bring in the energy of each color to chakra and the aura. Other methods include using Reiki to heal each chakra by simply placing your hands over the area. Because chakras are considered wheels of energy, the healer can use a pendulum allowing the pendulum to spin over each chakra. The pendulum will move over the chakra and stop when the adjustment is finished. Some people use their hands going counterclockwise to clean out the "gunk" or to slow a speeding wheel. Then you can spin the chakra clockwise to speed it up. Everyone senses differently when a wheel is balanced. I hear a "hum" with what I call my "third-ear" (similar to a third eye, but for sound) when a chakra is balanced.

Each chakra has a color, seed sound, associations, organ(s) and a picture. The number of petals of the lotus, or padma, for every wheel is different. As one moves up the chakras, each represents a higher vibration and function. The first chakra corresponds to the transcendence of matter. The first three chakras represent the most basic human needs. The fourth chakra, when opened, allows the ability to direct Prana, performs healings and transcends the limited self. The fifth chakra is the first of the higher centers. The sixth chakra is the first of the two major head chakras and the certainty of eternal nature as well as the existence of the Divine. The seventh chakra is the connection to the Divine and the destination of an ascended Kundalini.

FIRST CHAKRA

By meditating thus on Her who shines within the Muladhara chakra, with the luster of ten million Suns, a man becomes Lord of speech and a king among men, and an Adept in all kinds of learning.

—Verse 13, *Sat-Cakra-Nirupana*
in Naomi Ozaniec, *Chakras for Beginners,* 1994.

CHAKRA	First or Root Chakra; Muladhara; "Root Support"
COLOR	Red
SEED SOUND	Lam
KEYWORDS	Elemental earth, survival, instinct, rootedness, a sense of belonging, growth, biology, nature
ORGANS & FUNCTION	Adrenals (generates fight or flight response) and excretion
LOTUS PETALS	Four

SECOND CHAKRA

He who meditates on this stainless lotus, which is named Svadisthana, is freed immediately from all his enemies.

—Verse 18, *Sat-Cakra-Nirupana*

in Naomi Ozaniec, *Chakras for Beginners,* 1994.

CHAKRA	Second or Sacral Chakra; Svadisthana; "One's own abode"
COLOR	Orange or vermilion
SEED SOUND	Vam
KEYWORDS	Elemental Water, intimacy, relationships, sharing, sexuality, reproduction, the unconscious, ideas, imagination
ORGANS & FUNCTION	Reproductive system, urinary tract, womb, menstrual cycle, testes, prostatic plexus.
LOTUS PETALS	Six

THIRD CHAKRA

Meditate there on the regions of Fire, triangular in form and shining like the rising sun.

—Verse 20, *Sat-Cakra-Nirupana*

in Naomi Ozaniec, *Chakras for Beginners,* 1994.

CHAKRA	Third or Solar Plexus Chakra; Manipura; "Filled with jewels"
COLOR	Yellow
SEED SOUND	Ram
KEYWORDS	Elemental Fire, self-determination,
ORGANS & FUNCTION	Autonomy, purpose, destiny, will power, self-empowerment, prana. Digestion, liver, spleen, stomach, small intestines.
LOTUS PETALS	Ten

Fourth chakra

This lotus is like the celestial wishing tree.

—Verse 26, *Sat-Cakra-Nirupana*
in Naomi Ozaniec, *Chakras for Beginners,* 1994.

CHAKRA	Fourth or Heart Chakra; Anahata; "Unstruck"; Abode of Mercy
COLOR	Green and pink
SEED SOUND	Yam
KEYWORDS	Elemental Air, transpersonal love, universal compassion, unconditional love, limitless, infinite
ORGANS & FUNCTION	Heart, circulation, lungs
LOTUS PETALS	Twelve

Fifth chakra

This region is the gateway of the great Liberation for him who desires the wealth of Yoga and whose senses are pure and controlled.

—Verse 30, *Sat-Cakra-Nirupana*
in Naomi Ozaniec, *Chakras for Beginners,* 1994.

CHAKRA	Fifth or Throat Chakra; Vishuddi; "To purify"
COLOR	Blue
SEED SOUND	Ham
KEYWORDS	Chakra Spirit, Akasa, creativity, communication, will-power, self-expression, direct talking, sound, vibration
ORGANS & FUNCTION	Respiration, thyroid, throat, jaw, teeth, mouth
LOTUS PETALS	Sixteen

SIXTH CHAKRA

The lotus names Ajna is like the moon, beautifully white.

—Verse 32, *Sat-Cakra-Nirupana*

in Naomi Ozaniec, *Chakras for Beginners,* 1994.

CHAKRA	Sixth or Brow Chakra; Ajna; "To know" and "To command"
COLOR	Indigo
SEED SOUND	Om
KEYWORDS	Intuition, far seeing, direct knowing, vision, transcendence
ORGANS & FUNCTION	Pituitary Gland, Mind, Brain, Eyes, and Cognition
LOTUS PETALS	Twenty

SEVENTH CHAKRA

Wise men describe it as the abode of Vishnu, and righteous men speak of it as the ineffable place of knowledge of the Atma, or the Place of Liberation.

—Verse 49, *Sat-Cakra-Nirupana*

in Naomi Ozaniec, *Chakras for Beginners,* 1994.

CHAKRA	Seventh or Crown Chakra; Sahasrara; "Abode of Shiva" or "Mystical Union"
COLOR	Violet or white
SEED SOUND	None
KEYWORDS	Enlightenment, self-realization, fulfillment, completion, samadhi, mysticism, cognition
ORGANS & FUNCTION	Connection to the Divine, the goal of the ascended Kundalini
LOTUS PETALS	Thousandfold

Notes—Chakra Therapy

Estes, C. *Women Who Run With the Wolves: Myths and Stories of the Wild Woman Archetype.*
New York: Ballantine Books, 1992.
Ozaniec, N. *Chakras for Beginners.* London: Headway-Hodder & Stoughton, 1994.

CHAPTER 5

CRYSTAL HEALING

Fashion a breastpiece for making decisions—the work of a skilled craftsman. Make it like the ephod: of gold, and of blue, purple and scarlet yarn, and of finely twisted linen…Then mount four rows of precious stones on it. In the first row there shall be a ruby, a topaz and a beryl, in the second row a turquoise, a sapphire and an emerald; in the third row a jacinth, an agate and an amethyst; in the fourth row a chrysolite, an onyx and a jasper. Mount them in gold filigree settings. There are to be twelve stones, one for each of the names of the sons of Israel, each engraved like a seal with the name of one of the twelve tribes.

—Exodus 28:15–21.

Crystals are made up of water with minerals in them. The minerals create different colors in the crystals. Each crystal has its own energy and use. As mentioned in previous chapters the stones can be matched by color to the corresponding chakra. The Greenfire healers are given a small bag with colored stones for use in crystal and chakra healings. Clear quartz crystals can be used on all chakras if you do not have a colored stone.

There are a variety of ways to cleanse your crystal. A crystal can be cleansed and charged by holding it in your hands and using Reiki. Running water over your crystal works, if it has a point wash it with the point down. Some people put their stones in sea salt; just make sure you never use the salt, but throw it out when you are done. Not all stones can be put in salt. If the stone is soft the salt will eat away at the crystal. One can charge a crystal by putting it outside on the ground, out in the sun or moon. Sometimes to cleanse and charge my crystals I will put them in the garden to sit out in rainstorms and the weather. I once purchased a crystal in a museum shop that was dead; it had no energy. I put it outside for months and let it sit. Eventually, it was full of energy. Smudge can be used to cleanse crystals, as can herbal sprays. Reiki the spray before putting it on your crystal for extra "zing." If you don't have a garden or potted plants outside you can always put your crystal in a window for charging and cleansing.

> By working consciously with the mineral kingdom, you learn how to better express your own inner light while helping the crystals to express theirs. We are on this earth together to serve each other, that each may grow, and in doing so, work in greater harmony to create a better world.
> —Katrina Raphaell, *Crystal Enlightenment* 1985.

Programming a crystal

There are a variety of ways to program a crystal. Because the Greenfire women are also Reiki practitioners, they can use the symbol Hon-She-Zhe-Sho-Nen on the crystal to cleanse it of all previous programming or energies. From there they can put their intention for its use into the crystal. Crystals are like energy magnifiers so ethical and moral behavior is extremely important when programming your crystal. We try to work for the highest good at all times, believing in the Threefold Law of what you send out comes back to you three times. If you program a crystal with ill intent this rule, I believe, will be magnified also. If you choose to use crystals for healing you can program this intention into them. Cleanse and charge a crystal using a method of your choice, then use Hon-She-Zhe-Sho-Nen to clean it of all other energies. Holding it in your hands ask the crystal to help you with a particular work, when you are finished, seal it with Cho-Ku-Rei.

> The quartz crystal is considered the strongest power object of all among such widely separated peoples as the Jivaro in South America and the tribes of Australia. Peoples as distant from one another as the aborigines of eastern Australia and the Yuman-speakers of southern California and adjacent Baja California consider the quartz crystal "living," or a "living rock." The widespread employment of quartz

crystals in shamanism spans thousands of years. In California, for example, quartz crystals have been found in archaeological sites and prehistoric burials dating as far back as 8,000 years.

—Michael Harner, *The Way of the Shaman*, 1990.

GRIDS

Crystal grids can be used to continuously send out an intention. You can match colors and stones to what you need. They can be as elaborate as you wish. A basic grid can be just clear quartz with a large stone in the middle and smaller stones can be placed around the center crystal with the points facing out. The stones can be programmed for a specific use. If you wish to send a constant message of healing for a person you can use Hon-She-Zhe-Sho-Nen to clear the stones and then picture the person healed and happy. Cho-Ku-Rei seals your work so you can use this to finish your programming. Grids can be set up throughout your home. Charging the crystals and programming them to protect your home is always a beautiful way to create a large grid.

Have you ever listened carefully to hear a special secret from a very important friend? That is how you open your mind and heart to communicate with crystals and healing stones. Drop any preconceived notions, expectations, or fears that it cannot be done, and allow the inner mind to receive the subtle impressions that the crystal will emanate. Open yourself to the possibility that these crystalline life forms want to share their secrets and wisdom with you. Accept without doubt the spontaneous images that come into consciousness. As the mind is trained to listen and communicate in silence, responses will come quickly and clearly as the light and energy of the stones you are working with reflect your own wisdom back to you.

—Katrina Raphaell, *Crystal Enlightenment*, 1985.

USES

Crystals can be used for sacred space, calling the quarters or your angels. They can be used to put at each direction to hold and amplify sacred space. My crystal teacher always suggested sleeping with a new crystal to get to know it and find out what it was meant to tell you. I find that most of my crystals "whisper" to me and I feel I did not get a restful sleep; instead I was up all night conversing with a friend.

Some people insist on buying perfectly polished crystals. Many of my crystals, like my pets, are the unwanted or "not as fancy" variety. I find that they give more to me because they have dents and scratches. Plus, they are just more affordable. It is for this same reason that I will buy a self-healed crystal. These crystals have extra knowledge about healing that they bring to a meditation or healing session. I have heard that some healers have had crystals for years that continue to heal and grow on their own from the energy of the Reiki. I believe this could happen.

Crystals can be used during meditation for protection, peace, and assistance with concentration. They can also be used for astral travel. A crystal elixir can be made by putting a crystal in a jar or outside of the container for a period of seven days. The elixir is preserved with a small amount of alcohol such as brandy or vodka. Be sure the crystal is not a soft or toxic crystal should you decide to put it in the water. The elixir can be used as a spray or ingested. Plants enjoy crystals and you can always put them by your plants for a mutual energizing relationship. Cars can be protected with crystals also. (Melody, 1995.)

> "It is a responsibility to work with a Record Keeper. The information received may be unlike anything you have witnessed or experienced. Data may be stored in them that has absolutely nothing to do with physical life on planet Earth. The person receiving the information must not only train their mind to be open to receive inconceivable concepts, but also must be capable of pro-advanced training. These crystals can transport the consciousness into higher dimensions and greater realities. The purpose…is to incorporate higher knowledge, wisdom, peace and love onto our planet."
>
> —Katrina Raphaell, *Crystal Enlightenment*, 1985.

CONFIGURATIONS

Below is a list of some common forms a person might come across when purchasing or using a crystal.

Clusters: Wonderful for group energy, enhancing the peace or harmony of the family, social and business groups.

Double-terminated: These crystals have points or terminations on each end of the stone.

Elestial: Natural terminations and over-growth of crystals including layers of crystals are attributes of this type of stone.

Gateway: A portal going through a crystal; often seen in calcite, amethyst, and fluorite. Can be used to gain access to other worlds, akashic records, as well as past and future lives.

Generator: The terminated apex is formed by a group of crystal faces all joining at the top of each crystal in the same place.

Key: A six-sided shape on the face or side of a crystal that gets narrower as it goes within the stone.

Manifestation: A smaller crystal is totally enclosed within a larger crystal.

Phantom: An image of another crystal within a stone, it can be white or colored.

Rainbow: A rainbow can be seen within the crystal.

Record Keeper: This crystal has raised triangles on the face of the stone.

Self-healed: Shows a scar where the crystal broke and then "healed," continuing to grow.

Teacher: A large stone with smaller stones around the base. Used to give knowledge or to "teach" its keeper.

Twin: These crystals are recognized by two or more growing together and are parallel to each other. (Melody, 1995.)

Window: A diamond on the face of a crystal that is connected to the line that leads to the termination.

CRYSTAL	COLOR	CHAKRA	HEALING USE	METAPHYSICAL USE	ENERGY
Clear quartz, Witch's Mirror	Clear	Crown	Body-mind connection, heals negativity, crown chakra, use on any chakra	Protection, healing, psychism, and power	Projective and receptive, Sun, Moon, Fire, Water, The Great Mother
Amethyst	Purple	Crown	Spirituality, contentment, heart, stomach, skin, teeth, skeletal, digestion, nervous system	Dreams, overcoming alcoholism, peace, love, protection against thieves, courage, and happiness	Receptive, Jupiter, Neptune, Water, Bacchus, Dionysus, Diana
Sodalite	Indigo	Third Eye	Rational, logical, intellectual thinking, lungs, multiple sclerosis, headaches, endocrine balance	Promotes wisdom, clears old patterns, access sacred laws of the Universe	Receptive, Venus, Water
Lapis Lazuli	Blue/ Indigo	Throat	Blood, heart, throat, incest recovery, eyes, epilepsy, infections, pain, fever and nervous system	Psychic development, self-knowledge, stone of total awareness, courage	Receptive, Venus, Water, Isis, Venus, Nut

CRYSTAL	COLOR	CHAKRA	HEALING USE	METAPHYSICAL USE	ENERGY
Turquoise, Venus Stone, Horse-man's Talisman	Green/ Blue	Heart/ Throat	High blood pressure, inflammation, lungs, breast milk, heart disease, wounds, burns, and headaches	Protection, protection from falls for horseback riders, prosperity, love, karmic love, money, and luck	Receptive, Venus, Neptune, Earth, Buddha, Hathor, and Great Spirit
Citrine	Yellow	Solar Plexus	Bladder, kidneys, liver, colon, eating disorders, and allergies	Protection, color work, psychic and sexual energy, trance states, studying, writing, prevent nightmares, wealth, creativity	Projective, Sun, Fire, removes fear
Carnelian	Orange	Sacral	Sexual organs, liver, gall bladder, pancreas, allergies, colds, neuralgia	Dispel depression, anger, rage, and jealousy, kundalini energy, protection from mind readers, strengthens astral vision, protects	Projective, Sun, Fire, and courage
Smoky quartz	Black	Root/ hand and foot chakras	PMS, digestion, elimination, quit smoking, drug issues	Connection to Earth, heals Yin-Yang energy, meditation, mood elevator	Grounding, Earth, receptive

Notes—Crystal Healing

Cunningham, S. *Cunningham's Encyclopedia of Crystal, Gem, and Metal Magic.* St. Paul: Llewellyn Publications, 1997.

Harner, M. *The Way of the Shaman.* New York: HarperCollins Publishers, 1990.

Holy Bible, Revised Standard Version, Book of Exodus. Chicago: International Council of Religious Education, 1928.

Melody. *Love is in the Earth: A Kaleidoscope of Crystals.* Wheat Ridge: Earth-Love Publishing House, 1999.

Raphaell, K. *Crystal Enlightenment: The Transforming Properties of Crystals and Healing Stones.* Santa Fe: Aurora Press, Inc., 1985.

Rea, J. *Patterns of the Whole, Vol. I: Healing & Quartz Crystals: A Journey with our Souls.* Boulder: Two Trees Publishing, 1987.

Stein, D. *The Women's Book of Healing.* St. Paul: Llewellyn Publications, 1987.

CHAPTER 6

HERBAL CRAFT

"Everywhere in creation [trees, plants, animals, and precious stones] there are mysterious healing forces, which no person can know unless they have been revealed by God"…Hildegard calls the healing force itself viriditas. Viriditas literally means greenness, growing energy, the principle of life and sexuality. Life from God transmitted into plants, animals, and precious stones is viriditas.
— Wighard Strehlow and Gottfried Hertzka,
Hildegard of Bingen's Medicine, 1988.

Wise Woman Craft incorporates the use of herbal medicines in its practice. The traditional method is called the simpling method; the herbal medicine is the simple. The reason for this term was the use of only one herb in the mixture. A person who created these concoctions was called a simpler. When a woman comes to Greenfire to study she is expected to work with one herb, thus making simples. Later as she becomes more proficient she can mix the herbs for a desired effect. It is important to take an herb singularly at first to make sure you have no ill effects and to learn how well it works on you. When a person takes herbs in combination and has a reaction to the mixture, they have no idea which herb they might be reacting to.

Many of the medicines we use today are derived from plants. Digitalis, the heart medicine, is an example of this; the medicine is created from the foxglove plant which is quite poisonous. The story about digitalis is that a village wise woman used the plant to heal and help people with heart problems.

There was a formally trained doctor who knew of this wise woman's success and wanted her recipe. He hounded her until out of frustration he killed her. Some stories say he accused her of being a witch and had her executed. Either way she never gave him the recipe. In an attempt to take her place as a healer, he used digitalis and killed several people before he figured out how much to use.

Many people think, mistakenly, that because herbs are natural they are harmless. This can be a dangerous mistake. Herbs should be grown, harvested and used with respect; a wise woman should use them with reverence. When using herbs one should also be mindful of any medicines the client is taking. This means if a person is taking MAO inhibitors, anything for moods, anxiety, or mental illness, they should not take St. John's wort because the medicine will not work as well. St. John's wort also decreases the effectiveness of birth control pills. The same goes for echinacea and antibiotics. If someone is taking medicine that affects the liver or they have liver disease, there are certain herbs that should not be considered because they are toxic to the liver. Comfrey is such an herb. Many garden grannies drink garden comfrey freely and swear by it. But because of the warning regarding comfrey we do not recommend it to those with liver issues. Needless to say it is important to do your research and understand how to use the herb, what the precautions are, and to approach them with respect.

The wise woman approach to herbal medicines is a shamanic approach. While we must understand the traditional values and uses of the herbs, we also commune with each plant. To truly understand a plant's energy we must "sit" with it. So when a woman comes to Greenfire they are told to find an herbal ally and "sit" with it. Of course the first question is, "What's an herbal ally?" The next question is, "What do you mean by sit with an herb?" An ally is an friend, so an herbal ally is a plant friend. Most of the women I work with choose a plant that will heal some ailment they have. They are required to grow it, harvest it, eat it, drink it, tincture it, and put it in an oil (if it can be used that way). Then they must sit with it, as in next to it, singing to the plant. They should Reiki the plant, speak with the herb, thank it for its gifts and listen to it.

The traditional way to harvest a plant is to ask permission, explain its use to the herb and after cutting it, give thanks. Some people offer tobacco or a piece of hair. Sending Reiki to the plant is also another way to giving thanks.

Some women have difficulty choosing what herb they will work with. I often suggest putting out a request before meditation or sleep. Reading about the herbs helps, as well as deciding what a person would be taking the herb for.

When harvesting herbs we pay attention to the moon phase and the season. Aerial parts (above the ground) of a plant should be harvested during a waxing moon. If you read the *Farmer's*

Almanac you will find the same suggestion. There have been tests done that show there are more alkaloids in the aerial parts of plants during a waxing moon. (Weed, 1985.) To harvest roots, one should wait until the first frost and dark of the moon because the energy as well as the nutrients have gone into the root. Try not to harvest a plant after it blooms because the energy has gone into the flower. Exceptions would be flowers such as lavender and plants such as mugwort.

> There are many people to whom the idea of using herbs (which can be bought dried, or otherwise skillfully prepared, by those who cannot gather them wild, as I do) to treat the ailments of their dogs appears nonsensical, or impossible. Yet my previous canine herbals, first published at my own expense because of the prejudices of orthodox veterinary medicine, have sold in their thousands. They have not sold because of literary merit or appeal to those who buy herbal books for "quaint" country lore and "amusing" extracts from old works; they have sold because every book has meant cures in a widening circle of success, convincing orthodox veterinary surgeons throughout Europe and America.
>
> —Juliette de Bairacli Levy, *The Complete Herbal Handbook*
> *for the Dog and Cat*, 1992.

DRYING HERBS

When harvesting an herb for drying, cut it during the morning on a sunny day. To catch the leaves or blossoms, put it in a paper bag. The best way to dry the plant is to put it in the trunk of your car, periodically shaking the bag. If you have a warm dry area to hang the herbs upside down, use string or a rubber band to secure the bunches. To catch any leaves or stems, use an old door or window screen under the hanging herbs to catch the pieces that fall off. When the plants are completely dry, break up the herbs and keep them in jars. To preserve them, keep the herbs in a cool dark place away from moisture. Whole, dried herbs last two years; cut, dried herbs last one year; and powdered herbs last six months. Any of the unused leftovers should be returned with thanks to the earth on the compost pile.

> Many reports have surfaced recently about the dangers of herbal medicine. Even perfectly benign plants such as chamomile and peppermint are finding themselves on the "herbal blacklist." Are we just now discovering the dangers of herbs? No—but

we are able to ingest herbs in tremendously potent forms. In the past, herbs were most often taken as teas, tinctures, and syrups. But herbal capsules, which make it easy for us to swallow as much herb as we wish, and standardized preparations, which contain extracts of herbal constituents that are far more concentrated than nature ever intended, have not been available until recently.... Don't be scared off from herbal medicine by a few dramatic news stories. Use your head. Herbs are powerful medicine, but they don't always have the same effect on everyone. Take the time to get to know the herbs and how they affect you; you'll reap the benefits of energy, health, and vitality for years to come.

—*Rosemary Gladstar's Family Herbal*, 2001.

We follow the Wise Woman tradition, so we use parts for measurement. I save old jars for my tinctures and I use vodka as my menstruum (liquid). If you are opposed to using alcohol and prefer to use glycerin or glycerate, the method is the same. On a sunny morning harvest your herbs, explaining to them what you want to use them for, and give thanks after you have harvested them. I find that the herbal combinations I prepare are often more effective than what I buy. I believe that part of that is the intention put into the work. By speaking to the plants and telling them what work needs to be done, by asking permission and giving thanks, the herbs are energized.

Utilizing the simpling method, fill half a jar with your plant material and fill the jar up with your choice of menstruum (liquid: vodka or glycerin.) Susun Weed says to check your vodka levels a day or two after you put the tinctures up, because the fairies will take a sip, and add a little more if needed. (Weed, 1992.) I use a spurtle which is similar to a long pestle to mash my herbs a little getting them under the liquid and releasing the oils. To label the jars I write what I put in it, the date and the moon phase. I tape this to the outside of the jar. Clear strapping tape works well because it makes a waterproof seal on the label, in case there are leaks or drips. The tincture should sit in a cool dark place for six weeks.

Twelfth-century herbal invocation

Earth, divine Goddess, Mother Nature who generates all things and brings forth anew the sun which you have given to the nations; Guardian of sky and sea and of all gods and powers... through your power all nature falls silent and then sinks in sleep. And again you bring back the light and chase away night and yet again you cover us most securely with your shades. You do contain chaos infinite, yea and winds and showers and storms; you send them out when you will and cause the seas to roar; you chase away the sun and rouse the storm. Again when you will you send forth the joyous day and give the nourishment of life with your eternal surety; and when the soul departs to you we return. You are indeed duly called Great Mother of the Gods; you conquer by your divine name. You are the source of strength of nations and of gods, without you nothing can be brought to perfection or be born; you are Great Queen of the Gods. Goddess! I adore thee as divine; I call upon your name; be pleased and grant that which I ask of you, so shall I give thanks to thee, Goddess, with due faith.

Hear, I beseech you, and be favorable to my prayer. Whatsoever herb your power does produce, give, I pray, with goodwill to all nations to save them and grant me this my medicine. Come to me with your powers, and howsoever I may use them, may they have good success to whosoever I may give them. Whatever you grant, may it prosper. To you all things return. Those who rightly receive these herbs from me, please make them whole. Goddess, I beseech you, I pray as a suppliant that by your majesty you grant this to me.

Now I make intercession to you all your powers and herbs and to your majesty, you whom Earth parent of all has produced and given as a medicine of health to all nations and has put majesty upon you, I pray you, the greatest help to the human race. This I pray and beseech from you, be present here with your virtues, for She who created you has Herself promised that I may gather you into the goodwill of him on whom the art of medicine was bestowed, and grant for health's sake good medicine by grace of your powers. I pray grant me through your virtues that whatsoever is wrought by me through you may in all its powers have good and speedy effect and good success and that I may always be permitted with the favor of your majesty to gather you into my hands and to glean your fruits. So shall I give thanks to you in the name of the majesty which ordained your birth.

—Original translation from "Early English Magic and Medicine," by Dr. Charles Singer. *Proceedings of the British Academy, Vol. IV.*, 1920.

Herbal vinegars

Herbal vinegars are a great way to take in minerals that herbs offer. Apple cider vinegar is a healthy choice to use. Harvest your fresh herbs and fill half the jar with them, the rest with vinegar. It will be ready in six weeks.

> Gather all Leaves in the hour of that Planet that governs them...Let your Medicine be something of the Nature of the Sign ascending.
> —Nicholas Culpeper, *The Complete Herbal*, 1653.

Herbal infusions

Herbal infusions are stronger than a tea. Depending on the herb, they should usually sit at least 30 minutes to 8 hours before being consumed. An herbal infusion can last 72 hours in the refrigerator. Large jars are great for making your infusion. After filling the jar with the herbs and water, just cap it and let it sit for the required period of time. For leaves and flowers the proportions are 1 ounce of the herb to 1 quart of water. Roots, barks, seeds, and berries should be in the proportion of 1 ounce of herb to 1 pint of water. Roots and barks should infuse for a minimum of 8 hours, whereas leaves should infuse for a minimum of 4 hours. Flowers take a maximum of 2 hours to infuse, and seeds or berries should not infuse more than 30 minutes maximum. (Weed, 1992.)

> ...I am forever encouraging people who are seeking well-being and health to daily brew their pot of herbs. Though useful for short-term health problems, herb teas are most effective for chronic health problems. Used consistently over an extended period of time, herb teas ensure gradual but steady long-term results. Since the menstruum (the substance used to extract the plant constituents) used is water, it is nontoxic and user-friendly.
> —Rosemary Gladstar, *Herbal Healing for Women*, 1993.

The Spirit of the plants has come to me
In the form of a beautiful dancing green woman
Her eyes filled me with peace
Her dance filled me with peace
The spirit of the plants has come to me
And has blessed me with great peace
Her eyes filled me with peace
Her dance filled me with peace
The spirit of the plants has come to me
In the form of a beautiful dancing green woman
—Lisa Thiel, *Journey to the Goddess*, 1984.

OILS AND SALVES

Put the herbs in the jar, not quite filling it to the top. Pour olive oil over the herbs, stopping about ¼ inch from the top. Using a chopstick, press down on the herbs, releasing the air bubbles, then fill the rest of the jar and cap it. For the first two weeks, every few days, open the jar, press out the air bubbles and add more oil, capping tightly again. It is best to store the jar in a cool, dark place on a tray or dish because of leakage. Also, labeling the lid, instead of the jar, can be helpful, too. The herbs should sit for six weeks before straining. Piercing a vitamin E capsule and squeezing it into the oil will act as a natural preservative. If you have a very large jar, use more capsules.

To create a salve, use a teaspoon of beeswax for every ounce of strained oil. Heat the oil on the stove on a low flame. Take the oil off the flame when it starts to bubble and add the beeswax, then 3 drops of vitamin E oil for every 2 ounces. The salve will be spreadable with 1 teaspoon in it; if you prefer a harder salve, add up to 2 teaspoons of beeswax. Pour the hot, liquid salve into a jar and let cool.
—Judith Berger, *Herbal Rituals*, 1998.

The nine herbs charm

Forget me not, mugwort, what thou didst reveal

What thou didst prepare at Regenmeld

Una, you are called oldest of herbs.

Thou has strength against three and against thirty

Thou hast strength against poison and against infection

Thou hast strength against the foe who fares through the land!

And thou plantain, Mother of herbs

Open from the East, might within

Over three chariots creaked, over three queens rode

Over three brides made outcry

Over three bulls gnashed their teeth.

All these thou didst withstand and resist

So mayest thou withstand poison and infection

And the foe who fares through the land!

This herb is called watercress and it grew on a stone

It resists poison, it fights pain

It is called harsh, it fights against poison

This is the herb that strove the snake

This has strength against poison

This has strength against infection

This has strength against the foes who fare through the land!

Now, garlic, conquer the great poisons, though thou are the lesser

Thou, the mightier, vanquish the lesser until he is cured of both!

Remember, chamomile, what thou didst reveal

What thou didst bring to pass at Alford:

That he never yielded his life because of infection

After chamomile was dressed for his food!

This is the herb which is called nettle

The seal sent this over the back of the ocean

To heal the hurt of the other poison!

These nine sprouts against nine poisons

A snake came crawling, it bit a man

Then Woden took nine glory-twigs

Smote the serpent so that it flew into nine parts.

There the apple brought his to pass against poison

That she nevermore would enter her house!

Thyme and fennel, a pair of great power

Woden, holy in heaven

Wrought these herbs while he hung on the tree

He placed and put them in the seven worlds to aid all, the poor and rich.

It stands against pain, resists the venom

It has power against three and against thirty

Against a fiend's hand and against sudden trick

Against Witchcraft of vile creatures!

Now these nine herbs avail against nine evil spirits

Against nine poisons and against nine infectious diseases

Against the red poison, against the running poison

Against the yellow poison, against the green poison

Against the black poison, against the dark poison

Against snake blister, against water blister

Against thorn blister, against thistle blister

Against ice blister and against poison blister

If any poison comes flying from the east or any comes from the north

Or any from the west or south upon the peoples

—Saxon Herbal known as *The Lacnunga*,
Silver Ravenwolf, *American Folk Magick*, 1999.

Notes—Herbal Craft

Berger, J. *Herbal Rituals: Recipes for Everyday Living.* New York: St. Martin's Press, 1998.

Culpeper, N. *The Complete Herbal.* Bel Air: Book Jungle, 1653.

Gladstar, R. *Herbal Healing for Women.* New York: Fireside, 1993.

Gladstar, R. *Rosemary Gladstar's Family Herbal: A Guide to Living Life with Energy, Health, and Vitality.* North Adams: Storey Books, 2001.

Levy, J. *The Complete Herb al Handbook for The Dog and Cat.* London: Faber and Faber Limited, 1992.

Ravenwolf, S. *American Folk Magick: Charms, Spells and Herbals.* St. Paul: Llewellyn Publications, 1999.

Singer, C. *"Twelfth Century Herbal Invocation."* Original translation from *Early English Magic and Medicine, Vol. IV.* London: Proceedings of the British Academy, H. Milford, Oxford University Press, 1920

Strehlow, W. & Hertzka, G. *Hildegard of Bingen's Medicine.* Santa Fe: Bear & Company, 1098/1988.

Thiel, L. *Journey to the Goddess.* Monrovia: Sacred Dream Productions, 1995.

Weed, S. *Wise Woman Herbal for the Childbearing Year.* Woodstock: Ash Tree Publishing, 1985.

Weed, S. *Menopausal Years, The Wise Woman Way.* Woodstock: Ash Tree Publishing, 1992.

CHAPTER 7

AROMATHERAPY

Henna with nard, nard and saffron, calamus and cinnamon, with all trees of frankincense, myrrh and aloes, with all chief spices...Awake, O north wind and come, O south wind! Blow upon my garden, let its fragrance be wafted abroad.

—Song of Solomon 4:14–16.

WHAT IS AROMATHERAPY?

Aromatherapy is the inhalation and application of essential oils from aromatic plants, grasses, bark, roots, trees and flowers to restore or enhance health and beauty. It produces a physical, spiritual, emotional and mental sense of well-being. Aromatherapy works on various levels through the skin, as in massage and it combines this with the inhalation of different scents. The essential oils used in aromatherapy are derived from plants and chosen for their therapeutic and magical properties. Aromatherapy is an intensely comforting and reassuring healing therapy which has become extremely popular. The basic intention of aromatherapy is to bring together the scientific achievements of man with his intuitive understanding for the treatment of illnesses with the most effective and useful therapy. (Worwood, 1996.) The principle of aromatherapy is to strengthen the self-healing processes by preventative methods and indirect stimulation of the immune system. Aromatherapy is an ancient and popular approach to total well-being that is in tune with nature. Essential oils have been effectively used around the world for centuries for therapeutic purposes such as fighting infection, strengthening the immune system, reducing emotional or mental stress, as well as providing a basis for preventative medicine. (Worwood, 1999.)

Since ancient times aromatherapy has been utilized. There are pictures on the walls of caves in France of flowers and plants. Their essences have been used for healing, for relaxation and as an aphrodisiac. Ancient peoples captured the magic of different fragrances, creating an art that can do anything from calm to strengthen. It is a science based on nature and it affects the entire being, mind, body and spirit. Holistic healing is an increasing consciousness in today's society and is widely accepted. In ancient Egypt, aromatherapy was a way of life. (Schiller & Schiller, 1994.) In *Magical Aromatherapy*, Scott Cunningham explains, "On the walls of ancient tombs and temples lost in the desert, one symbol frequently occurs—a half-round, handled object with lines representing smoke rising from it." (Cunningham, 2004.) This validates the use of incense in Egypt form the earliest times. The scents of specific plants were used during religious rituals, because certain smells could raise higher consciousness or promote a state of tranquility, just as incense is still used in services today. (Worwood, 1996.)

In his work *Natural History,* Pliny recorded the recipe for an Egyptian perfume used during Graeco-Roman times. "Metopium" consisted of cardamom, rush, reed, honey, wine, myrrh, galbanum and terebinth, as well as other ingredients. Egyptians had not discovered distillation yet, so they soaked plants in oils or fats; the oil would absorb the scent slowly. (Cunningham, 2004.) Egyptians understood the principles of this and incorporated it into their cooking as well. Specific herbs aided in the digestive process, protected against infection, or built the immune system. Aromatherapy became medicinal when the Greeks took medicine to a new level. Hypocrites, the "Father of Medicine," was the first to study cause and effect. These studies led him to believe that daily aromatic baths and scented massages would promote good health. Oils scented with quince or white violet eased stomach upset. Grape-leaf perfume was used to clear the head and a garland of roses was for a headache. (Cunningham, 2004.) Holistic practitioners today follow the same belief. The Greeks believed that the fresh scents rising from living plants maintained physical health. Their houses were constructed with rooms that opened onto herb and flower gardens. (Cunningham, 2004.) Megalus, a Greek perfumer, created a scent known a Megaleion. It included cinnamon, myrrh and burnt or charred frankincense that were soaked in oil of balanos.

The Romans carried the use of perfumes to such an extravagant extent that even scented earthenware cups were popular. These were created by soaking the cups with perfume prior to use. In 565 a law was passed which forbade the use of exotic scents by private citizens due to a fear that there wouldn't be sufficient incense to burn on the altars of the deities. In this Roman document, there were scents suitable to specific deities: laurel and savin were recommended for invoking every deity, ambergris to Venus, cassia and benzoin to Jove, as well as costus to Saturn. (Cunningham, 2004.)

As people migrated across Europe, they carried with them the knowledge of benefits of specific herbs and oils of their native lands. China, India and some Arab nations kept a greater understanding of the use of herbs, where medicine was studied more than in medieval Europe. The Renaissance and the discoveries of the great explorers introduced new aromas. The twentieth century brought a new enlightenment to this ancient art. During the turn of the century, French chemist and author Dr. Gattefosse brought a renewed interest in aromatherapy. (Worwood, 1996.) He studied and documented essential oils and their healing properties. He discovered that different applications had antiseptic, anti-inflammatory and antiviral effects. He experimented with these discoveries on soldiers during World War I. These applications were carried on to World War II. Now today, yet more studies show how the use of essential oils promotes good total health. (Schiller & Schiller, 1994.)

WHAT ARE ESSENTIAL OILS?

Essential oils are highly concentrated extracts of flowers herbs, grasses, shrubs and trees. These tiny droplets are found in particular glands, hairs or specific structures of the plant and contain some of the active principles of the plant. Similar to the herbal therapy principles, are phytochemicals with particular biological properties. Non-oily in texture, these highly concentrated substances are obtained by steam distillation, peel pressure and solvent extraction methods. Only the utmost quality of essential oils should be used in aromatherapy. (Worwood, 1991.) Scott Cunningham explains their energy, "Because essential oils are born of plants, they have a direct link with the Earth. This subtle energy, nourished by soil, sun and rain, vibrates within essential oils. Since we too are of the Earth and also possess this link, we can merge the energy of true essential oils with our own to create needed change." (Cunningham, 2004.) Pure essential oils are usually sold in small amounts and range in price from inexpensive to costly.

While most people will buy their oils, some make them. Juliette de Bairacli Levy makes oils from eucalyptus, camphor, lavender, rosemary, thyme, rue, lemon balm, rose and wormwood. One can mince the herbs with a machine, however Juliette prefers to pound them with a pointed stone on a hollow stone. Two tablespoons of the ground herbs are added to a half-pint bottle which is then filled three-quarters full with a fine oil such as sunflower or corn oil and a tablespoon of vinegar. The oils should be placed in the hot sunlight for three weeks and shaken daily. To make a strong oil, every five days the oil should be strained, the old herbs pressed of the oil and new ground herbs should be added for the three week period. (Levy, 1997.)

How do essential oils work?

Essential oils work in harmony with the body to balance it. They produce certain effects that we can count on, but can also adapt to the needs of different people. Used for their anti-microbial and antiseptic effects, essential oils are not only less toxic than synthetic antibiotics, but are also eubiotic (support life) by working with the body's own natural healing abilities. Certain oils, such as Roman chamomile, promote cell regeneration, are antiseptic and have wound healing effects, as well as having anti-fungal and anti-inflammatory properties, making them the ultimate active principles for holistic natural skin-care. (Worwood, 1996.)

What are the effects of oils?

Oils can directly or indirectly affect the physiological systems. Used topically for their antiseptic and soothing effects, essential oils can successfully treat minor skin conditions. It has been shown that the application of certain essential oils to the skin can produce vasodilation, which causes warming of underlying muscles. In addition, because of the effect of relaxation on the brain and the subsequent sedating or stimulating of the nervous system, essential oils can also indirectly raise or lower blood pressure as well as aid in normalization of hormonal secretion. Essential oil can have effects on emotions and mental states. Perception of odors can have a major impact on memory, learning, emotions, thinking and feeling. As therapeutic agents, essential oils work similarly to tranquilizers but in a subtle, organic way. Most scents uplift spirits and calm the nervous system. (Schiller & Schiller, 1994.)

Essential oils' effect on the body and mind

The sense of smell is 10,000 times more sensitive than any of the other senses. The human nose is capable of distinguishing between hundreds of thousands of different odors. Without the sense of smell, our capabilities to enjoy food or sex are greatly diminished. Smell is the only sense in which the receptor nerve endings are in direct contact with the outside world. The olfactory nerve is an extension of the brain itself, reached directly through the nose. This nerve is a direct link to our emotions, memory and learning. Essential oils trigger an olfactory nerve impulse, which goes directly to the brain and produces aromatherapy's far-reaching effects. Researchers in France have found that due to this process when women in labor smell lavender, their pain is greatly diminished. Other research has found that when men put baby powder behind their ears it works as an aphrodisiac, whereas if women put cinnamon behind their ears men find the same effect for them. (Worwood, 1991.)

How are essential oils used?

Inhalation is most useful for respiratory symptoms and can be done by sniffing drops on a tissue or by inhaling near a diffuser. Local application of diluted oils (2-10% in a vegetable oil base like grapeseed oil) on various points such as spinal nerves, chakras, meridians and pulse points is effective for certain conditions. Full-body massage is quite effective; it can provide relaxation as well as a physiological action through the nervous system. (Schiller & Schiller, 1994.)

It is important to incorporate common sense and knowledge when utilizing essential oils for particular medicinal results, as many are irritating or sensitizing as well as photo-toxic. Aromatherapy provides health and body care on a completely natural basis and the subtle qualities of the oils lend themselves best to a gradual experience. The combination of factual information available coupled with a developed intuition makes one capable of generating great successes in self-healing. Using essential oils is pleasant; eventually this experience then grows into a heightened awareness of increased health as a consequence of external use of essential oils. (Worwood, 1994.)

Massage

This is the most effective method of using the oils, combining their properties with the therapeutic power of touch. The oils should be diluted with odorless carrier oil, such as grapeseed, sweet almond, jojoba or peach kernel. A dilution of three percent essential oil to carrier oil is a recommended starting point; use less if the person has sensitive skin. This is approximately 1-6 drop(s) essential oil in three teaspoonfuls of carrier oil. Swedish massage is the most popular massage used with aromatherapy, because oil is usually used which facilitates the stroking and kneading of the body, stimulating metabolism and circulation. Its active and passive movements of the joints promote general relaxation, improve circulation, relieve muscle tension and increase the range of motion. Swedish massage is often given as a complete, full body technique, though sometimes only a part of the body is worked on. Another method is acupressure. (Worwood, 1994.) Both Swedish massage and acupressure are based on applying pressure with the finger and palm using a pattern of specific points. The goal is the efficient and balanced flow of *chi* through the meridians.

It is believed that where there is tension being held in the body, the flow of *chi* is impaired through those areas, which can lead to chronic problems not only in the muscles but also in the associated organs. Reflexology is massage of the feet or hands. Aromatherapy works great with this type of massage also. (Worwood, 1996.)

Massage oil recipes

The drop equivalent is 1-10 drops of oil to 1 tablespoon (15 milliliters). Always use a carrier oil when using essential oils; never use them undiluted. Some common carrier oils are sweet almond, grapeseed, jojoba, olive and sesame. All of these recipes are combined with 1-2 tablespoons of carrier oil. If you are working on children, dilute the essential oils further. If you are making a mist, just omit the oil and add to 4 ounces of water and double the recipe. (Wharton, 2009.)

Recipes for specific needs	Oil and number of drops
Communication	Frankincense 4 drops Geranium 4 drops Ylang ylang 3 drops
Fatigue	Bergamot 4 drops Pine 4 drops
Happiness	Sandalwood 4 drops Lavender 2 drops Orange 1 drop
Headache relief	Peppermint 5 drops
PMS relief	Lavender 4 drops Ylang ylang 4 drops Geranium 2 drops
Pain reliever	Eucalyptus 5 drops Pine 5 drops
Reflexology mix	Peppermint 4 drops Lavender 4 drops Rosemary 2 drops

Recipes for specific needs	Oil and number of drops
Romance blend	Ylang ylang 4 drops
	Patchouli 2 drops
	Orange 2 drops
Stress reliever	Lavender 3 drops
	Rosewood 3 drops
	Sandalwood 2 drops
Uplifting	Lemongrass 5 drops

BATHS

Using oils in baths is a simple, effective and pleasant way to relax as well as receive the thera-peutic effects. Water has therapeutic value, which enhances the powers of the oils. To use, add 6–10 drops of essential oil or a blend of oils to the surface of the water. Add no other substances, then soak for about 20 minutes while inhaling the vapors.

COMPRESSES

Add 5–10 drops of essential oil to 1 quart of warm water, then soak a piece of clean cotton in the water, wring out and place the cloth on the affected area. (Wharton, 2009.)

SPIRIT OF LAVENDER RECIPE

2 tablespoons dried lavender flowers (rosemary, basil, or other aromatic herbs can be used)

1 tablespoon grated nutmeg or mace

2 teaspoons cinnamon (or 1 teaspoon of cinnamon and 1 teaspoon of clove)

1 tablespoon of sweet cecily (if available)

Pulverize and mix well, then add a quart of pure grain alcohol. Let steep in a warm spot, such as a sunny window, for 2 weeks shaking daily. When the spirit of lavender is ready, strain off herbs and put in a bottle that you can cap tightly. Excellent on cold wet cloths to soothe headaches or fevers by placing on the forehead. Can also be placed on pulse points of wrist for fevers. This tonic can be used internally for mental depression and nervous ailments by taking on a sugar cube. (Levy, 1997.)

Inhalation

Add 5–10 drops of essential oil into a bowl of steaming water, then place a towel over your head and the bowl and inhale the vapor for a few minutes. This is great for colds and sinus congestion.

Vaporization

All essential oils are antiseptic and evaporate easily, so they make very good air-fresheners. For example, relaxing sandalwood or clary sage is good for parties; peppermint clears your mind when you need to work. There are many different types of vaporizers from the simple bowl of water on the radiator with a few drops of oil on the surface, to vaporizer light bulb rings or specially made vaporizer bowls which sit above candle holders. (Wharton, 2009.)

Perfumes

After bells had rung
And were silent…
Flowers chimed
A peal of fragrance

What bloom on what tree
Yields
This imperceptible
Essence of incense?
—Basho, late seventeenth century

You can make your own perfume by blending different oils. Try experimenting with different combinations, which can be mixed with a carrier oil or non-fragrant alcohol. A diluent is an unscented alcohol and glycerin that is mixed with the essential oils. If you wish to make these into oils for the bath, just replace the diluent with almond oil or an oil of your preference. (Riggs, 1992.)

Perfume	Oils & drops
A fruity and spicy scent.	Cassis 60 drops Vetiver 9 drops Cinnamon 6 drops Pine balsam 6 drops Diluent to fill a quarter-ounce bottle
A honey-sweet fragrance known as a chypre, for the island of Cyprus. See recipe on page 57.	Oakmoss 24 drops Bergamot 18 drops Amber 12 drops Vetiver 12 drops Pine balsam 6 drops Diluent to fill a quarter-ounce bottle
A floral and fruity scent.	Sandalwood 24 drops Orange blossom 20 drops Rose 12 drops Cinnamon 8 drops Rosemary 4 drops Lemongrass 4 drops Diluent to fill a one-ounce bottle
An old fashioned fragrance with violets and hints of green.	Violet 40 drops Heliotrope 12 drops Vetiver 8 drops Juniper 4 drops Lilac 4 drops Diluent to fill a quarter-ounce bottle
Ambergris enhances a woman's natural scent. A sensual perfume.	Ambergris 40 drops Jasmine 16 drops Musk 8 drops Frankincense 4 drops Diluent to fill a quarter-ounce bottle

Perfume	Oils & drops
An oriental blend, with a sweet, rich fragrance.	Patchouli 18 drops Vanilla 9 drops Amber 9 drops Orange blossom 30 drops Jasmine 18 drops Diluent to fill a quarter-ounce bottle
A sensuous, musky, scent with a blending of rose.	Rose 40 drops Rose geranium 30 drops Sandalwood 12 drops Musk 4 drops Diluent to fill a quarter-ounce bottle
A spicy amber fragrance, with the underscent of cedarwood lifting slowly from the skin.	Bergamot 30 drops Carnation 18 drops Sandalwood 18 drops Patchouli 12 drops Cedarwood 6 drops Diluent to fill a quarter-ounce bottle
A green scent with hints of blossoms.	Lavender 30 drops Rosemary 8 drops Tuberose 20 drops Oakmoss 16 drops Diluent to fill a one-ounce bottle
Green, fruity and exotic scents blend well in this perfume.	Cassis 30 drops Frangipani 20 drops Patchouli 14 drops Gardenia 12 drops Ylang-ylang 4 drops Cedarwood 4 drops Diluent to fill a quarter-ounce bottle (Riggs, 1992.)

POUDRE DE CHYPRE

Macerate oak moss in water, steeping it for several days. Press this with a cotton cloth and moisten it with rosewater and one-third orange flower water until the moss has absorbed this fully. Press the moss again with the cotton cloth and pulverize it. This is used as a basis for other perfumes and increases their powers. (Levy, 1997.)

QUEEN OF HUNGARY WATER

3 cups spirit of rosemary

1 cup spirit of lavender

4 ounces of rose water

Let stand in a warm place for several days. Then shake 15 minutes, bottle and cap tightly. Can be used for fevers, headaches or to soothe nerves. This is a wonderful skin toner for your face. (Levy, 1997.)

SKIN CARE

The following is a list of oils for skin care; they are shown according to skin types.

- *Normal skin*: Lavender, palmarosa, geranium, chamomile, rosewood, benzoin. Any of these can be mixed with hazelnut oil.
- *Dry skin*: Sandalwood, rosewood, lavender, patchouli, geranium, chamomile. These can be combined with jojoba, sesame or avocado oil.
- *Oily skin*: Ylang-ylang, lemon, lime, orange, lavender, juniper. These can be combined with grapeseed oil.
- *Problem skin*: Myrrh, lavender, geranium, chamomile, sandalwood, rosewood. Kukui nut oil is recommended for this skin type.
- *Sunburn relief*: Lavender and aloe gel. (Wharton, 2009.)

CHAKRAS AND AROMATHERAPY

Below is a list of the seven main chakras and the oils associated with them. The oils may be mixed with a carrier oil and placed directly on the chakra centers, or put on stones and placed on the body. (Wharton, 2009.)

- *Crown*—Frankincense—Quartz
- *Third Eye*—Lavender—Amethyst

- *Throat*—Eucalyptus—Turquoise
- *Heart*—Ylang Ylang—Rose Quartz
- *Solar Plexus*—Pine—Tigers Eye
- *Navel*—Patchouli—Carnelian
- *Root*—Myrrh—Red Jasper

CRYSTALS AND AROMATHERAPY

These are crystals and essential oils you can use together during rituals.

- Amber and frankincense for strength, healing and protection.
- Amethyst and yarrow for love and psychic awareness.
- Aquamarine and eucalyptus for health, healing and purification.
- Bloodstone and black pepper for courage and physical energy.
- Carnelian and cardamom for sex and overcoming sexual dysfunction.
- Chrysoprase and neroli for happiness and joy.
- Clear calcite and sandalwood for spirituality and meditation.
- Fluorite and lavender for healing, health and conscious mind.
- Green tourmaline and patchouli for money.
- Imperial topaz and niaouli for protection.
- Kunzite and ylang-ylang for love and peace.
- Lapis lazuli and palmarosa for love and healing.
- Lepidolite and cedarwood for spirituality, sleep and protection.
- Malachite and pine for magical energy, money and protection.
- Moonstone and jasmine for love, sleep and psychic awareness.
- Quartz crystal and rosemary for all positive magical changes.
- Red jasper and juniper for protection.
- Red tourmaline and geranium for protection.
- Rhodochrosite and ginger for physical energy and love.
- Rose quartz and rose for love, peace and happiness. (Cunningham, 2004.)

DAYS OF THE WEEK AND THEIR SCENTS

Day	Planetary Ruler	Aroma
Monday	Moon	Jasmine, lemon, sandalwood, stephanotis
Tuesday	Mars	Basil, coriander, ginger, nasturtium
Wednesday	Mercury	Benzoin, clary sage, eucalyptus, lavender
Thursday	Jupiter	Clove, lemon balm, oakmoss, star anise
Friday	Venus	Cardamom, palmarosa, rose, yarrow
Saturday	Saturn	Cypress, mimosa, myrrh, patchouli
Sunday	Sun	Cedar, frankincense, neroli, rosemary (Cunningham, 2004.)

SEASONS AND THEIR SCENTS

Season	Scent
Spring	Daffodil, jasmine, rose; all sweet scents
Summer	Carnation, clove, ginger; all spicy scents
Autumn	Oakmoss, patchouli, vertivert; all earthy scents
Winter	Frankincense, pine, rosemary; all resinous scents (Cunningham, 2004.)

LUNAR CYCLES AND THEIR CORRESPONDING SCENTS

Moon phase	Scent
First Quarter	Sandalwood
Full Moon	Jasmine
Last Quarter	Lemon
New Moon	Camphor (Cunningham, 2004.)

Choosing and storing oils

Essential oils are affected by sunlight, therefore they should be sold and stored in dark glass bottles, with stopper caps. Make sure that the cap is on securely and the bottle is stored in a cool dark place. Never store essential oils in plastic bottles. Good essential oils should keep for several years if properly stored, although the oils of orange, lemon and lime will not keep as long. Patchouli is at the other extreme and actually gets better as it ages. For quality, just remember: you get what you pay for.

Mixing essential oils

Use a dropper so that you can measure the actual number of drops easily. Use a different dropper for each oil or rinse it out with very hot water to avoid cross contamination. Good internal droppers have a groove on one side. With the groove uppermost you will get a "slow drip," with the groove downward you will get a "fast drip." (Wharton, 2009.) Place the base oil in a glass container, then add the essential oils according to their suggested amounts. To blend the oils, swirl them around in the container; do not stir. If blending with a specific intention, swirl the oil clockwise for increase and counterclockwise for decrease. (Cunningham, 2004.)

Carrier oils

The following carrier oils can be used with your essential oils:

Almond	Olive	Apricot kernel	Palm	Grapeseed
Safflower	Hazelnut	Sesame	Sunflower	Jojoba

To preserve your oils, add vitamin E or wheat germ oil. Only jojoba oil does not need a preservative because it is actually a liquid wax and does not become rancid. Never use mineral oil. (Cunningham, 2004.) Jojoba oil, if properly stored, has a 100-year shelf life, which may be a consideration when mixing oils. Keep in mind that jojoba is very expensive. It is the closest thing to your skin, the sebum and is very safe for most humans and pets. (Ravenwolf, 2006.)

Essential oils and properties

Here is a list of some oils on the market today. There are hundreds out there, but some are rare and very hard to find. Most of these are easily accessed at health and nutrition stores as well as the Internet. Some oils are very reasonably priced, others, like jasmine, rose and Melissa, can be costly but well worth it because just one drop is enough. (Wharton, 2009.)

When working with essential oils keep in mind that the scents cause very personal responses. Where one person might love a scent, another might find that it evokes a different reaction for them. Pay attention to your reaction to particular scents and those of your clients. If a scent doesn't smell nice to the person using it there is no sense including it in a blend. Also be aware of allergic reactions to oils. (Cunningham, 2004.)

Allspice (Pimento): Its aroma resembles a mixture of pepper, clove and cinnamon. This oil is stimulating and vitalizing. It has been used to treat depression, nervous exhaustion, arthritis, fatigue, stiffness, flatulence and indigestion. It is debatable whether it should be used in massage since it is such a powerful oil, because it may irritate the skin and mucous membranes. This is a very warming oil that gets the circulation going. It blends well with frankincense, ginger, lemon and orange.

Aloe (Aloe barbadensis): This oil has a light fresh fragrance. Aloe lessons pain. It is healing and rejuvenating for skin or hair. (Wharton, 2009.)

Anise (Pimoinella anisum): It has a spicy, warm, licorice-like aroma. Anise is well known for its effect on the digestive system. It may have a good effect on asthma, breathing difficulties and sexual problems, such as impotence or frigidity. Anise is said to control lice and is good for infectious skin diseases. It blends well with fennel, petitgrain and rosewood. (Wharton, 2009.)

Balsam (Myroxylon pereirae): It used as an anti-infective and soothes chafed skin. Balsam has an exotic aroma that anchors and strengthens, imparting a rich, earthy scent to perfumes. Use with caution as it is a skin sensitizer. (Wharton, 2009.)

Basil, Sweet (Ocimum basilicum): This oil has a warm, fiery scent. It is good for tired, overworked muscles, as a mouthwash for mouth sores and infected gums, for chest infections as well as digestive problems. Basil blends well with bergamot, lavender, neroli and verbena. *Magickal uses and associations:* conscious mind, happiness, peace, money, Mars and Fire. In the sixteenth century John Gerard said, "The smell of basil taketh away sorrowfulness and maketh a man merry and glad." (Cunningham, 2004.)

Bay (Larus nobilis): It has a light, spicy, sweet aroma. Bay may act as an appetite stimulant, settles stomach pains. It is used for general aches and pains, as well as rheumatic pains. Bay blends well with rose, cedarwood and eucalyptus. *Magickal uses and associations:* Psychic awareness, purification, bringing in positive changes, money, Sun and Fire.

Benzoin (Styrax benzoin): Benzoin has a cinnamon-vanilla like scent. It is warming to the body, reduces stress, is calming and mood uplifting, and breaks up congestion. Benzoin works well with spicy scents. *Magickal uses and associations:* Physical energy, magickal energy, conscious mind, Mercury and Air.

Bergamot (Citrus bergamia): This oil has an uplifting, spicy, sweet scent, like orange and lemons with floral overtones. Inhaled, it relaxes the nervous system, acts as a digestive, an expectorant, antidepressant and antiseptic. Bergamot blends well with chamomile, lavender, neroli and geranium. Bergamot is a photosensitizer (increases the skin reaction to sunlight and makes it more likely to burn) and the photosensitizing effect can last for several days. (Wharton, 2009.) *Magickal uses and associations:* Peace, happiness, restful sleep, prosperity, protection, Sun and Fire. (Cunningham, 2004.)

Birch, sweet (Betula alba): Birch a powerful oil which could irritate sensitive skin. It is best used with caution or not at all. This oil has an invigorating, even rousing effect on the spirits and stimulates the sweat glands, aiding the body in releasing harmful toxins. Birch is a lymphatic cleaner and helps keep infection at bay. Its diuretic properties could also help with obesity and cellulitis. This oil could be good for rheumatism and muscle pain generally since it eliminates accumulation of uric acid in the joints. Birch blends well with chamomile, frankincense and lemon. (Wharton, 2009.) *Magickal uses and associations:* Birch is associated with the Goddesses Freya and Cerridwen. In Ogham, the Celtic writing system, Beithe was the symbol for the birch tree and meant new beginnings or youth. In the Runic system, the birch tree was associated with the rune Berkana and is considered the rune of transformation. In Eastern European traditions the birch is considered the "Lady of the Woods."

Cajeput (Melaleuca leucadendron): It has a camphor fragrance. Cajeput relaxes muscles, relieves aches and pains. (Wharton, 2009.)

Camphor (Cinnamomum camphora): This oil has a fresh, clean and very piercing scent. It is an analgesic, antidepressant, antiseptic, antispasmodic, diuretic, stimulant, laxative and vermifuge. Camphor is a very powerful oil; overdosing could cause convulsions and vomiting. It should be avoided in pregnancy as well as by people suffering from epilepsy and asthma. Camphor sedates nervy types, particularly when associated with depression. It raises low blood pressure, warms and cools the body where necessary. It is good for constipation, diarrhea and gastroenteritis. Camphor may be helpful with stiff muscles and reduces inflammatory conditions. It blends well with basil and chamomile. (Wharton, 2009.) *Magickal uses and associations:* Purification, physical energy, celibacy, Moon and Water. Camphor trees guard Taoist and Buddhist temples throughout China. (Cunningham, 2004.)

Caraway (Carum carvi): Caraway has a minty scent. It is a muscle relaxant, relieves pain and improves digestion. It blends well with eucalyptus and rosemary. (Wharton, 2009.) *Magickal uses and associations:* Physical energy, conscious mind, love, Mercury and Air. (Cunningham, 2004.)

Cardamom (Elettaria cardamomum): It has a spicy scent. Cardamom is a muscle relaxant, skin conditioner and soothing agent that is stimulating and toning. It blends well with geranium, juniper berry and lemon. (Wharton, 2009.) *Magickal uses and associations:* Love, sex, Venus and Water. (Cunningham, 2004.)

Carrot Seed (Daccus carota): Carrot seed oil has a slightly sweet and dry aroma. It is used to treat jaundice and other liver disorders. This oil is recommended for mature skin and wrinkled skin. It blends well with bergamot, lemon, orange and rosemary. (Wharton, 2004.)

Cassia (Cinnamomum cassia): Cassia has a cinnamon-like aroma. It is used to stimulate the pancreas. This oil blends well with all the spice and citrus oils, geranium and black pepper. (Wharton, 2009.) *Magickal uses and associations:* Physical energy, prosperity, psychic awareness, Sun and Fire. (Cunningham, 2004.)

Cedarwood (Cedrus atlantica; Atlas): Cedarwood has a sweet woody aroma which improves as the oil ages; it is a dark, amber, viscous liquid. Some of its properties are antiseptic, antiseborrheic, astringent and aids in the removal of body fat. It can be used externally for cellulite. Cedarwood blends well with bergamot, clary sage, frankincense, oakmoss and rosemary. (Wharton, 2009.) *Magickal uses and associations:* Spirituality, self-control, Sun and Fire. (Cunningham, 2004.)

Cedarwood, Virginia (Juniperus Virginiana-Red Cedar): This oil has a sweet cedar, woody aroma, reminiscent of sandalwood. It is not considered a true cedarwood as is Atlas. Cedarwood calms nervous tension and states of anxiety; it is an expectorant and it dries phlegm. This oil blends well with bergamot, cinnamon, frankincense, rose and rosemary. *Magickal uses and associations:* Spirituality, self-control, Sun and Fire. (Cunningham, 2004.)

Celery (Apium graveolens): This essential oil has a spicy scent. It is stimulating and toning.

Celery blends well with basil, cajeput, chamomile, grapefruit, lemon, orange, palmarosa and rosemary. (Wharton, 2009.) *Magickal uses and associations:* Psychic awareness, sleep, Mercury and Air. (Cunningham, 2004.)

Chamomile, German and Roman (Matricaria chamomilla/Anthemis nobilis): Both these have a fruity, apple-like aroma and contain azuline, a powerful anti-inflammatory. German chamomile has slightly more azuline and is a deeper blue color. Both oils have analgesic, antidepressant, antirheumatic and sedative properties. They blend well with bergamot, jasmine, palmarosa, rose and ylang ylang.

Cinnamon, cinnamon leaf (Cinnamon zeylanicum): This oil has a spicy, sharp and sweet aroma. It is used as an insecticide, an antispasmodic and an aphrodisiac. Cinnamon eases colds as well as breathing difficulties, and it freshens breath. It is very powerful and should be used with extreme care as it is a skin irritant. It blends well with clove, frankincense, lavender, orange and thyme. *Magickal uses and associations:* Physical energy, prosperity, psychic awareness, Sun and Fire. (Cunningham, 2004.)

Citronella (Cymbopogon nardus): This oil has a slightly sweet and lemony aroma. It is used as an insecticide and an antidepressant. Its most useful quality seems to be as an insect repellent, and it may also help pets get rid of fleas. Citronella is also known to clear the mind, so it may be useful against headaches and migraines. It blends well with citrus oils, peppermint and eucalyptus.

Clary Sage (Salvia sclarea): This is a heavy, herbal and nutty fragrance. A relaxing, warming oil that eases nervous tension and soothes digestive problems. It is a hormone balancer and may regulate scanty periods. Clary Sage blends well with bergamot, lavender, lime and geranium. (Wharton, 2009.) *Magickal uses and associations:* Euphoria, calm, dreams, Mercury and Air. (Cunningham, 2004.)

Clove (Eugenia caryophyllata): Clove has a spicy and penetrating aroma that is highly irritating to the skin. It is beneficial to the digestive system, effective against diarrhea, vomiting and spasms. Clove can help toothaches, rheumatism, arthritis and mouth sores. It blends well with basil, cinnamon, citronella and orange. (Wharton, 2009.) *Magickal uses and associations:* Healing, memory, protection, courage, Jupiter and Fire. (Cunningham, 2004.)

Coriander (Coriandrum sativum): It has a slightly pungent, sweet and spicy aroma. This oil stimulates the mind, especially in the presence of fatigue and tension. Coriander may help memory, have some effect on bad breath, alleviate muscle spasms, and relieve stomach gas and cramps. This oil blends well with bergamot, lemon and jasmine. (Wharton, 2009.) *Magickal uses and associations:* Memory, love, healing, Mars and Fire. (Cunningham, 2004.)

Cypress (Cupressus sempervirens): Cypress has a woody and slightly spicy aroma. Its effect on varicose veins is well known. This oil regulates the menstrual cycle and soothes anger. It blends well with bergamot, lavender, lemon, pine and sandalwood. (Wharton, 2009.) *Magickal uses and associations:* Easing loses, healing, Saturn and Earth. (Cunningham, 2004.)

Eucalyptus (Eucalyptus globulus): This oil has a woody, lemon aroma. It is a very effective insect repellent due to a higher citronellal content than citronella. (Wharton, 2009.) *Magickal uses and associations:* Health, purification, healing, Mercury and Air. (Cunningham, 2004.)

Fennel (Foeniculum vulgare): Fennel has a floral, herby and slightly spicy aroma. It is an antiseptic, a diuretic, an insecticide and a laxative. It is an excellent body cleanser; it may rid the system of toxins from alcohol and excessive eating, making it great for hangovers. Fennel is a tonic to the digestion; it decreases appetite, is an antispasmodic, good for vomiting, colic, constipation and gas. This oil helps to increase milk flow in nursing mothers. It blends well with lavender, lemon, rose and sandalwood. (Wharton, 2009.) *Magickal uses and associations:* Longevity, purification, courage, Mercury and Air. (Cunningham, 2004.)

Fir Needle (Abies alab): This oil is clear and has a balsamic, refreshing aroma. It is an antiseptic, expectorant and sedative. That may have a beneficial effect on chest conditions, such as fluid and mucous. It helps with muscle aches. This oil blends well with basil, cedarwood and frankincense. (Wharton, 2009.)

Frankincense (Boswellia thurifera): Frankincense has a woody, spicy, incense-like scent. It is an antiseptic, diuretic, digestive and sedative. This oil is very helpful in clearing the lungs that eases shortness of breath. It may diminish effects of cystitis, genitourinary infections and heavy periods, acting as a tonic to the uterus. Frankincense soothes the stomach, easing belching. It blends well with basil, geranium, lavender, orange and sandalwood. (Wharton, 2009.) *Magickal uses and associations:* Spirituality, meditation, Sun and Air. (Cunningham, 2004.)

Geranium (Pelargonium graveolens): This oil is an antidepressant, antiseptic and insecticide. It calms anxiety, lifts the spirits and assists with depression. It is useful with premenstrual tension and may assist with menopausal problems such as vaginal dryness and heavy periods. Geranium assists with breast inflammation, helping to clear the body of toxins, which may also be helpful with addictions. It stimulates the lymphatic system, which keeps infections at bay. This oil eases neuralgia. It blends well with basil, bergamot, carrot seed, jasmine, lavender and rose. (Wharton, 2009.) *Magickal uses and associations:* Happiness, protection, Venus and Water. (Cunningham, 2004.)

Ginger (Zingiber officinale): Ginger has a spicy, woody and warm scent, with a hint of lemon. It is an antiseptic, analgesic, expectorant, laxative and aphrodisiac. Ginger aids memory, cheers one up and eases sore throats. It settles the digestive system, is effective against nausea, hangovers, jet lag, sea and travel sickness. Ginger relieves cramps, rheumatic pains and muscle spasms. It is a valuable remedy in cases of impotence. This oil blends well with cajeput, cinnamon, eucalyptus, frankincense, geranium, orange and verbena. (Wharton, 2009.) *Magickal uses and associations:* Magickal energy, physical energy, sex, love, money, courage, Mars and Fire. (Cunningham, 2004.)

Grapefruit (Citrus paradisi): It has a sweet, sharp, citrusy aroma. It is an antidepressant, antiseptic, diuretic and disinfectant. Grapefruit is invaluable in times of stress; uplifting and reviving the spirit. It may have an effect on obesity and fluid retention and could help with cellulite. It is a tonic to the liver. This oil relieves migraines, premenstrual tension and jet lag. It blends well with bergamot, cedarwood, frankincense and lavender. (Wharton, 2009.)

Hyssop (Hyssopus officinalis): This oil is has a warm, sweet, penetrating aroma. It is an antirheumatic, antiseptic, antispasmodic, astringent, cicatrizing (helps form a scar), digestive, diuretic, emmenagogue, expectorant, febrifuge (lowers a fever), emollient, hypertensive, nervine, sedative, stimulant, stomachache, sudorific (causes perspiration) and vermifuge. This very potent oil is recommended in low dosages, if at all. People who are expecting, or those who have epilepsy and high blood pressure should not use it. This oil clears the mind, gives a feeling of alertness; it cures grief by clearing the spleen. It raises low blood pressure and is very effective on respiratory problems, viral infections such as colds, coughs, sore throat, bronchitis and asthma, by liquefying mucous and relieving bronchial spasm. Hyssop acts as a mild laxative, relieves stomach cramps, expels wind and is said to get rid of worms. It is beneficial to the menstrual cycle, particularly with water retention during periods and is effective against amenorrhoea as well as leucorrhoea. This oil blends well with fennel, lavender and tangerine. (Wharton, 2009.) *Magickal uses and associations:* Conscious mind, purification, Jupiter and Fire. (Cunningham, 2004.) *Purge me with hyssop and I shall be clean; wash me and I shall be whiter than snow. (Psalms 51: 7-8.)*

Jasmine (Jasminum sambac/Jasminum grandiflorum/Jasminum officianale): Jasmine has a sweet, flowery and exotic aroma. It is called the "king of flower oils" because it has always had a reputation as an aphrodisiac, antidepressant, antiseptic, emollient and sedative. It is an excellent remedy for severe depression and it calms the nerves. This oil is effective in postpartum depression and promotes the flow of breast milk. Jasmine relieves spasm of the bronchi, calming irritating coughs. It blends well with bergamot, frankincense, rose, orange and sandalwood. (Wharton, 2009.) *Magickal uses and associations:* Love, peace, spirituality, sex, sleep, psychic dreams, Moon and Water. (Cunningham, 2004.)

Juniper (Juniperus communis): This oil has a refreshing and slightly woody aroma. It is an antiseptic, antispasmodic, aphrodisiac, diuretic and insecticide. It should not be used if there is any type of kidney or inflammatory problems. This oil is an effective diuretic and antiseptic of the genitourinary tract, making it very valuable in treating cystitis and kidney stones. It helps with cellulitis, clears intestinal mucous, treats gout and rheumatism, as it helps to eliminate uric acid. Juniper regulates periods and eases painful cramps. It blends well with bergamot, cypress, frankincense and sandalwood. (Wharton, 2009.) *Magickal uses and associations:* Protection, purification, healing, Sun and Fire. (Cunningham, 2004.)

Lavender, French (Lavandula officinalis): Lavender is analgesic, antidepressant, antirheumatic, antiseptic, antispasmodic, antiviral, bactericide, cicatrizant, decongestant, deodorant, diuretic, fungicide and sedative. It soothes the spirit and relieves anger, making it valuable in manic-depressive cases. This oil has a sedative action on the heart, assists in bringing down high blood pressure, relieves insomnia, and relieves muscular spasms and rheumatic pains. It is useful with menstrual problems, clears the spleen and the liver. Lavender may be useful in nausea, vomiting and colic. It keeps insects at bay as well as purifies the air. It promotes growth of new skin cells, having great healing effect on burns and sunburn, acne, psoriasis, boils, fungal growths and scarring. This oil blends well with bergamot, chamomile, citronella, lemon and pine. (Wharton, 2009.) *Magickal uses and associations:* Health, love, celibacy, peace, conscious mind, Mercury and Air. (Cunningham, 2004.)

Lemon (Citrus limon): This oil has a fresh, sharp citrus aroma. It is an antacid, antineuralgic, antirheumatic, antiseptic, astringent, bactericide, diuretic, emollient, insecticide and laxative.

Lemon helps to clear thoughts. It is a tonic to the circulatory system that liquefies the blood and aids the flow; thereby easing pressure on varicose veins. It is used to bring down high blood pressure and is helpful in nosebleeds. This oil eases painful cold sores, herpes, constipation and cellulite. It relieves headaches and migraines. Lemon soothes insect bites and stings. It blends well with chamomile, eucalyptus, lavender and rose. (Wharton, 2009.) *Magickal uses and associations:* Healing, health, physical energy, purification, Moon and Water. (Cunningham, 2004.)

Lemongrass (Cymbopogon citratus): This essential oil has a sweet and lemony aroma. It is an antidepressant, antiseptic, bactericide, diuretic, fungicide and insecticide that stimulates the mind and lifts the spirit. This oil stimulates the appetite; it is helpful with colic and indigestion. Lemongrass prevents the spread of contagious diseases and is great for aching muscles. It relieves tired legs, fatigue and assists with jet lag. This oil also aids in the flow of milk in nursing mothers. Lemongrass blends well with cedarwood, basil, lavender, neroli, niaouli and tea tree. (Wharton, 2009.) *Magickal uses and associations:* Psychic awareness, purification, Mercury and Air. (Cunningham, 2004.)

Lime (Citrus auranttifolia): Lime is very restorative. It is very stimulating in cases of apathy, depression and anxiety. This oil eases coughs and chest congestion, encourages appetite and may assist in anorexia. Lime assists in treating alcoholism because of its disinfecting and restorative properties. It blends well with bergamot, geranium, lavender, rose and ylang-ylang. (Wharton, 2009.) *Magickal uses and associations:* Physical energy, purification, protection, Sun and Fire. (Cunningham, 2004).

Mandarin (Citrus, reticulata): Mandarin has a citrus scent. It is a calming, soothing agent, astringent and skin conditioner. It blends well with basil, bergamot, chamomile, clary sage, geranium, grapefruit, lavender, lemon lime, rose, neroli and orange.

Marjoram, Spanish (Origanum margorana): Marjoram has a warm, penetrating and slightly spicy aroma. It is an analgesic, antiseptic, antispasmodic, digestive, expectorant, sedative and laxative. It calms the nervous system and may give a feeling of comfort in cases of grief as well as loneliness. Marjoram is very effective in dealing with painful muscles, mostly in the lower back area. It assists with swollen joints and it is good as an after-sports rub. This oil seems to lower high blood pressure, soothes digestion; it may help with stomach cramps, constipation, flatulence and seasickness. This oil alleviates nasal congestion during colds and may be useful in relieving painful periods. It blends well with bergamot, cedarwood, orange and rosewood. (Wharton, 2009.) *Magickal uses and associations:* Peace, celibacy, sleep, Mercury and Air. (Cunningham, 2004.)

Melissa (Melissa officinalis; Sweet Balm, Lemon Balm): This oil is distilled from lemon balm, it is true Melissa. Most of the Melissa essential oils offered are a mixture of lemon-scented oils, which might even include citronella; this oil is considered "the most adulterated essential oil in the industry." It takes approximately 1.5 tons of the plant to obtain a pound of true Melissa essential oil, thus the expensive price of this true, unadulterated essential oil. Its odor is uplifting and calming at the same time. This oil has proved useful for oily skin, acne, cold sores, herpes, fungal infections, chronic coughs, colds (with headache), slowing rapid breathing, lowering blood pressure, colic, nausea, indigestion, menstrual problems, regulating menstrual cycle, anxiety, depression, insomnia, migraine, tension and anger. It may irritate sensitive skin and should only be used in small dilutions (4–6 drops per ounce of carrier oil) and should be avoided during pregnancy. Always use in the lowest recommended concentrations. (Wharton, 2009.) *Magickal uses and associations:* Purification, peace, money, Jupiter and Air. (Cunningham, 2004.)

Myrrh (Commiphora myrrha): This oil has a smoky and slightly musky aroma. It is antiseptic, astringent, deodorant, disinfectant and diuretic. It is best avoided during pregnancy as it is an emmenagogue. Myrrh seems to lift feelings of weakness, apathy, lack of incentive and also has a cooling effect on heated emotions. Due to its drying action it is effective against excessive mucous in the lungs. It is recommended for use in cases of bronchitis, colds, sore throats and coughs. This oil is excellent for mouth, or gum disorders; it is the best treatment for mouth ulcers, gingivitis and bleeding or spongy gums. It eases flatulence and hemorrhoids. Myrrh stimulates and invigorates the immune system. It is of great benefit in cases of scanty periods, leucorrhea and clearing obstructions in the womb. This oil blends well with clove, frankincense, lavender and sandalwood. (Wharton, 2009.) *Magickal uses and associations:* Healing, spirituality, meditation, Saturn and Water. (Cunningham, 2004.)

Myrtle (Myrtus communis): This oil has a fresh, slightly sweet and penetrating scent. It is an antiseptic, astringent, bactericide and expectorant. Myrtle may soothe feelings of anger and is particularly useful with pulmonary disorders, especially when accompanied by night sweats. It combats excessive moisture, bronchial catarrh, clears sinusitis, eases hemorrhoids and diarrhea. Myrtle could stem leucorrhea; it is said to be an effective tonic to the womb.

This oil keeps vermin away. Myrtle could be useful in treatment of acne as well as clearing blemishes or bruises; it may also alleviate the scaling appearance of psoriasis. This scent blends well with coriander, lavender, rosemary and tea tree.

Neroli (Citrus aurantium; Orange Blossom, Orange Flower): This oil has a beautiful floral fragrance. It is an antidepressant, antiseptic, antispasmodic, aphrodisiac, deodorant, digestive and sedative. A very relaxing, rather hypnotic scent, this oil relieves chronic anxiety, depression and stress; it is good in cases of insomnia. It assists with nerve pain, headaches and vertigo, even bouts of yawning. Due to its calming effect, Neroli may be beneficial with sexual problems and is said to be an effective aphrodisiac. It may relieve menopausal symptoms of irritability and tearfulness. Due to its antispasmodic action, this oil calms the intestines, which can be helpful with colitis and diarrhea. It blends well with bergamot, geranium, jasmine, lavender, lime, rose and ylang ylang. (Wharton, 2009.) *Magickal uses and associations:* Purification, joy, sex, Sun and Fire. (Cunningham, 2004.)

Niaouli (Melaleuca virdiflora): This oil has a slightly sweet, penetrating aroma. It is an analgesic, antiseptic, bactericide, cicatrizant, insecticide and decongestant. Niaouli clears the head and may aid in concentration. It helps to fight infection by increasing white blood cell and antibody activity. Niaouli is excellent for chest infections, bronchitis, asthma and sinusitis. This oil may be effective in dealing with urinary infections. Due to its pain relieving properties, it may be of aid in rheumatism and neuralgia. This scent blends well with coriander, fennel, juniper, orange and peppermint. (Wharton, 2009.) *Magickal uses and associations:* Protection, healing, Mercury and Air. (Cunningham, 2004.)

Nutmeg (Myristica fragrans): Nutmeg has a spicy, warm and nutty odor. It is considered an analgesic and neurotonic. This oil is indicated for extreme tiredness and used in massage blends for aching joints. When this scent is inhaled it can cause nausea. One drop of nutmeg with 20–40 drops of orange is wonderful for the home. This oil blends well with citrus oils. (Wharton, 2009.) *Magickal uses and associations:* Physical energy, magickal energy, psychic awareness, money, Jupiter and Fire. (Cunningham, 2004.)

Oakmoss Absolute (Evernia prunastri): Oakmoss is a lichen, usually found growing on oak trees and sometimes on other species such as spruce and pine. It is a viscous liquid with an extremely intense aroma reminiscent of a damp forest floor. Its odor is uplifting, cooling and calming; it is reputed as an aphrodisiac. This oil has antiseptic and expectorant qualities. It is not advisable to use this oil for professional aromatherapy, but it can be used as a mood-enhancing skin perfume or environmental fragrance. Its properties are more emotional and spiritual than physical. It can irritate sensitive skin. This scent blends well with cedarwood, citrus, pine, floral and vetiver. (Wharton, 2009.) *Magickal uses and associations:* Money, Jupiter and Earth. (Cunningham, 2004.)

Orange, Sweet (Citrus aurantium): This oil is a zesty, refreshing citrus fragrance. It is an antidepressant, antiseptic, antispasmodic, digestive and sedative. Prolonged use and high dosage may irritate sensitive skin and there's a chance of phototoxicity on skin exposed to the sun. Orange relieves gloomy thoughts and depression, dispels stress and revives one when bored. It calms the stomach in nervous states, assists with diarrhea and constipation. It may encourage appetite; don't use if you are dieting. Orange seems to have a good effect on colds and bronchitis. It is very good for painful and sore muscles. This oil may relax insomnia brought on by anxiety and has a possibility of bringing down high level of cholesterol in the blood. It blends well with cinnamon, coriander, clove, frankincense, jasmine, lavender and rose. (Wharton, 2009.) *Magickal uses and associations:* Physical energy, purification, joy, magickal energy, Sun and Fire. (Cunningham, 2004.)

Oregano (Origanum vulgare): This has an herby, woody, yet slightly spicy scent. It is analgesic, antirheumatic, antispasmodic, antiseptic, disinfectant, emmenagogue, expectorant, laxative and stomachic. A very potent oil, oregano could irritate the mucous membranes. It is best avoided in pregnancy. Its main effect seems to be on the digestive system, soothing the stomach, liver, spleen and calming intestinal spasm. It may combat acidity and stomach gas and encourage appetite. Oregano alleviates symptoms of asthma and whooping cough. Its warming and pain relieving action may be beneficial to menstrual cramps, rheumatism and muscular pain. Apparently it has some effect on pediculosis (infestation by skin parasites). Oregano blends well with basil, fennel, geranium and pine.

Palmarosa (Cymbopogon martini): This oil is a bactericide and febrifuge. It refreshes and clarifies the mind. Palmarosa may be effective in cases of fever by reducing temperature. It acts as a tonic to the digestive system and stimulates the appetite, making it helpful in cases of anorexia nervosa. Palmarosa may ease stiff joints. It blends well with bergamot, citronella, jasmine, lavender, petitgrain and rose. (Wharton, 2009.) *Magickal uses and associations:* Love healing, Venus and Water. (Cunningham, 2004.)

Parsley Seed (Petroselinum sativum): This oil has a somewhat herby aroma with spicy undertones. It is an antiseptic, antispasmodic, aphrodisiac, digestive, expectorant, emmenagogue and laxative. Some precautions should be taken with this very powerful oil, dizziness may result. It should not be used in pregnancy or during painful menstruation as it may induce contractions of the womb. Parsley seed is best avoided in cases of kidney disease and peptic ulcers. It is debatable whether it should be used in massage. This oil is a very strong diuretic and stimulates the kidneys; it could effectively clear cystitis and urinary stones. It is rather useful in childbirth since it stimulates contractions during labor. Parsley seed could well promote flow of breast milk and seems to relieve hardening of the breasts. While having a calming action on the digestion, it also stimulates the appetite. It is useful for flatulence, and takes the sting out of insect bites. This oil clears wounds and bruises by stimulating the blood flow. It is good for keeping head lice away. This scent blends well with lavender, lime and orange. (Wharton, 2009.) *Magickal uses and associations:* Protection, Mercury and Air. (Cunningham, 2004.)

Patchouli (Pogostemon patchouli): This oil has a strong, earthy fragrance, which is sweet and spicy as well. It is an antidepressant, antiseptic, aphrodisiac, astringent, deodorant, fungicide and insecticide. This scent may cause loss of appetite. Its odor may be little too persistent for some people. Due to its strong astringent and cicatrizing properties, patchouli may be helpful for loose skin, especially after dieting. It is excellent in cases of diarrhea. Its diuretic properties are useful in cases of water retention and cellulite. Patchouli is well known to increase libido. It relieves effects from insect bites. It is known as a tissue regenerator, which helps the regrowth of skin cells and the forming of scar tissue. Patchouli heals rough and cracked skin. This scent blends well with black pepper, clary sage, frankincense, geranium, lavender and myrrh. (Wharton, 2009.) *Magickal uses and associations:* Physical energy, sex, money, Saturn and Earth. (Cunningham, 2004.)

Pennyroyal (Micromeria fruticosa): This essential oil should be used with extreme caution. Its scent is herbaceous and minty. It is a well known emmenagogue; do not use it during pregnancy. Pennyroyal has some use in menstrual difficulties and is often used to bring on menstruation. It's valuable in repelling insects on animals. This oil can be diluted either in alcohol or vinegar as a rub to kill fleas. Many aromatherapists will not use this oil. It blends well with cedarwood and peppermint. (Wharton, 2009.) *Magickal uses and associations:* Physical energy, conscious mind, protection, Mars and Fire. (Cunningham, 2004.)

Pepper, Black (Pioer nigrum): Black pepper has a sharp and spicy aroma. It's an analgesic, antiseptic, antispasmodic, aphrodisiac, cardiac, detoxicant, digestive, diuretic, laxative and stomachic. There's the possibility of skin irritation; too much too often may over stimulate the kidneys. It is very stimulating to the mind, giving stamina where there's frustration. It is useful for muscular aches and pains, and muscular stiffness, as it assists with dilation of local blood vessels. Black pepper is good to use before excessive exertion. It assists with rheumatoid arthritis and temporary limb paralysis. This oil stimulates appetite, expels wind, quells vomiting and restores tone to colon muscles. It banishes excess fat, possibly by aiding digestion of protein; it generally expels toxins. This oil may be helpful with anemia, as it aids in the formation of new blood cells. It can bring down high temperatures in very small amounts. Black pepper is helpful with bruises. This scent blends well with basil, bergamot, cypress, grapefruit, lemon and sandalwood. (Wharton, 2009.) *Magickal uses and associations:* Banishing. (Moura, 2007.)

Peppermint (Menthe pipefitter): This oil has a sharp and menthol fragrance. It is an analgesic, anesthetic, antispasmodic, astringent, decongestant, emmenagogue, expectorant, insecticide and stimulant. Peppermint should be kept away from eyes, because it is likely to irritate skin and mucous membranes. It is best avoided by pregnant women and nursing mothers as it may discourage flow of milk. This oil is said to relieve states of anger, hysteria and nervous trembling and is excellent for mental fatigue as well as depression. On the body, it has a dual action: cooling when hot and warming when cold. As a remedy for colds, it halts mucous and fevers, and encourages perspiration. Peppermint is extremely important for its effect on the digestive system and it has a slightly anesthetic effect on stomach muscles; making it good for travel sickness, vomiting, diarrhea, constipation, colic and nausea. Its stimulating qualities are useful for shock, vertigo, anemia and dizziness. Its cooling and pain relieving action seems to ease headaches, migraines and toothaches. Scanty menstruation, painful periods and mastitis could well respond to this oil. It can be used to repel insects and vermin. Peppermint blends well with cedarwood, cypress, lavender, neroli and pine. (Wharton, 2009.) *Magickal uses and associations:* Purification, conscious mind, Mercury and Air. (Cunningham, 2004.) .

Petitgrain (Citrus bigarade): This oil has a fragrance that is alternately woody and floral. It is an antidepressant, antispasmodic and deodorant. It calms anger and panic, refreshing the mind as well. Petitgrain eases breathing and relaxes muscle spasms. It is helpful with painful digestion by calming stomach muscles and could help in clearing up skin blemishes as well as pimples. This oil blends well with bergamot, cedarwood, lavender, neroli, orange, rosewood and sandalwood. (Wharton, 2009.) *Magickal uses and associations:* Conscious mind, protection, Sun and Fire. (Cunningham, 2004.)

Pine (Pinups sylvestris): Pine has a fresh, forest aroma. It is an antiseptic, decongestant, deodorant, diuretic, expectorant and sudorific. This oil is known to refresh a tired mind and is used for mental fatigue. It is a powerful antiseptic and helpful in cases of bronchitis, laryngitis and influenza. Pine has a good effect on respiratory problems. It is effective with cystitis, prostate problems and is a known as a general kidney cleanser. Its warming properties may relieve rheumatism, gout and arthritis, as well as muscular pain and stiffness. This oil is reputedly effective on male sexual problems and possible impotence. It blends well with cedarwood, clove, myrtle and niaouli. (Wharton, 2009.) *Magickal uses and associations:* Healing, purification, physical energy, magickal energy, protection, money, Mars and Air. (Cunningham, 2004.)

Rose Otto (Rosa centifolia/Rosa damascena): This oil has a deep, sweet, flowery and an exquisite perfume. It is also known as Damask Rose from Bulgaria. It is an antidepressant, antiseptic, antispasmodic, aphrodisiac, bactericide, diuretic, emmenagogue, laxative and sedative. Since it is an emmenagogue, it is best avoided in pregnancy. Rose has a soothing effect on the emotions, particularly depression, grief, jealousy and resentment. It lifts hearts and eases nervous tension as well as stress. This scent gives a woman positive feelings about herself. Rose helps with premenstrual tension, promotes vaginal secretions and regulates the menstrual cycle. Its beneficial action on infertility aids "male" problems also, probably by increasing the semen. This oil is helpful with sexual difficulties, particularly frigidity and impotence. The scent releases the "happy" hormone, dopamine. It activates sluggish blood circulation, relieving cardiac congestion and toning the capillaries. It relieves nausea, vomiting and constipation to some extent. This oil has a purging action on toxins; the Romans valued it for hangovers. Rose has a soothing action on sore throats and eases coughs. It is useful for all skin types, though particularly good for mature, dry, hard or sensitive skin. This oil is a valuable treatment for broken thread veins. It blends well with bergamot, chamomile, clary sage, geranium, lavender, orange and sandalwood. (Wharton, 2009.) *Magickal uses and associations:* Love, peace, sex, beauty, Venus and water. (Cunningham, 2004.)

Rosemary (Rosamarinus officinalis): This scent has a refreshing herbal fragrance. It is an analgesic, antidepressant, antirheumatic, antiseptic, antispasmodic, astringent, cicatrizing, digestive and diuretic. It is not suitable for people with epilepsy or high blood pressure. This oil should be avoided in pregnancy since it is an emmenagogue. Rosemary clears the head, aids memory, is good for mental strain and it revives the senses. This scent clears headaches and migraines, especially when connected to gastric problems. It may assist with vertigo. This essential oil helps to tone temporarily paralyzed limbs. It helps ease gout and tired, overworked muscles. Rosemary could ease colitis, flatulence and stomach pains. It seems to relieve menstrual cramps and scanty periods. Its diuretic properties may be useful with water retention during menstruation and may be effective with cellulite as well as obesity. Rosemary blends well with basil, cedarwood, frankincense, ginger, grapefruit, orange and peppermint. (Wharton, 2009.) *Magickal uses and associations:* Longevity, conscious mind, memory, love, Sun and Fire. (Cunningham, 2004.)

Rosewood (Bois de Rose; Aniba rosaeodora): This scent has a sweet, woody, floral and slightly spicy aroma. It is an analgesic, antidepressant, antiseptic, aphrodisiac, deodorant and insecticide. It is said to stabilize the central nervous system and could therefore have an overall balancing effect. This oil is helpful when feeling low and overwhelmed with problems. It may give a helpful boost to a lowered immune system. Its acclaimed aphrodisiac properties may work wonders in restoring libido and could have some effect on sexual problems such as impotence and frigidity. This oil is reputedly helpful for persons who have suffered sexual abuse. May relieve headaches when accompanied by nausea and may also relieve jet lag. Its deodorizing action helps the body cope with excess heat and moisture. This scent blends well with cedarwood, coriander, frankincense, rose, sandalwood and vetiver. (Wharton, 2009.)

Sage (Saliva officinalis): Sage is a camphoraceous; it is a soothing agent, energizing and stimulating. This scent blends well with rosemary and citrus oils. (Wharton, 2009.) *Magickal uses and associations:* Memory, conscious mind, wisdom, money, Jupiter and Air. (Cunningham, 2004.)

Sandalwood (Santalum album): This oil has a woody, sweet and exotic aroma. It is an antiseptic, antispasmodic, aphrodisiac, astringent, diuretic, expectorant and sedative. Its lingering aroma often persists in clothing after washing. Sandalwood should be avoided in states of depression as it may lower the mood even further. Its aphrodisiac properties are well known; it can relieve sexual problems such as frigidity and impotence. This oil alleviates cystitis (massage in the kidney region where it has a purifying and anti-inflammatory action.) Its antispasmodic action on the body should encourage relaxation. Sandalwood may have a cleansing action on the sexual organs as it was once used to alleviate sexually transmitted diseases. It could be useful in promoting vaginal secretions. This oil is helpful with chest infections and sore throats. It aids sleep during colds and flu, as it stimulates the immune system and keeps infection at bay. Sandalwood may also treat heartburn and may be helpful with diarrhea. It is particularly good for dry eczema as well as ageing and dehydrated skins. This oil relieves itching and inflammation. Sandalwood blends well with basil, black pepper, frankincense, geranium, lavender, lemon, neroli, rose and vetiver. (Wharton, 2009.) *Magickal uses and associations:* Spirituality, meditation, sex, healing, Moon and water. (Cunningham, 2004.)

Spearmint (Menthe spicata): Spearmint is very similar to peppermint but slightly sweeter. It is an antispasmodic, emmenagogue, insecticide and stimulant. If it is used in a full body massage, one should use only a minute amount, and massage in local areas may be preferable. There is a possibility of eye irritation, as well as sensitive skin and it should be avoided during pregnancy. Spearmint stimulates a tired mind. It is helpful with digestive problems such as vomiting, flatulence, constipation and diarrhea. This oil seems to relax stomach muscles, relieving hiccups and nausea, as well as seasickness. This oil releases retention of urine and apparently dissolves kidney stones. It controls the overabundance of breast milk as well as hardening of the breasts. Spearmint could stem the flow of heavy periods and leucorrhea and is said to promote easier labor during childbirth. This scent is good for headaches, bad breath and sore gums. It may help sores and scabs. Spearmint blends well with basil, grapefruit and rosemary. (Wharton, 2009.) *Magickal uses and associations:* Healing, protection during sleep, Mercury and Air. (Cunningham, 2004.)

Spruce (Picea mariana): This oil has a fresh pine, bitter orange aroma. It is recommended for relief of stress and anxiety. Spruce is also recommended for muscle aches, pains, aching joints, poor circulation and muscle spasms. It has been known to be helpful for bronchitis or asthma. This scent blends well with lavender and clary sage. (Wharton, 2009.)

Tangerine (Citrus tangelo): Tangerine has a sweet and tangy aroma. It is an antiseptic, antispasmodic, sedative and stomachic. This oil could be phototoxic; care should be taken not to expose the skin to strong sunlight after a treatment. It has an almost hypnotic effect on the mind. Tangerine may well be helpful with stress and tension due to its soothing action on the nervous system. It assists with gastric complaints, such as flatulence, diarrhea or constipation, stimulating the flow of bile which helps to digest fats. This oil assists with tired and aching limbs since it is a tonic to the vascular system. It could help smooth out stretch marks; particularly when blended with lavender and neroli. This scent blends well with basil, bergamot, chamomile, clary sage, frankincense, neroli, orange and rose. (Wharton, 2009.)

Tea Tree (Melaleuca alternifolia): This oil has a fresh and sanitary, rather pungent aroma. It is an antibiotic, antiseptic, antiviral, bactericide, cicatrizing, expectorant, fungicide, insecticide and sudorific. It may cause irritation on sensitive areas of skin; however, along with lavender, it is just about the only oil that is recommended to be used "neat" or straight from the bottle without dilution. It has a refreshing, revitalizing effect on the mind, especially after shock. Its most important usage is to help the immune system fight off infectious diseases; as it activates the white corpuscles to form a defense against invading organisms and helps to shorten the duration of an illness. Tea tree sweats toxins out of the body. It is indicated for influenza, cold sores and gingivitis. It is recommended for a series of massages before surgery as it will help to fortify the body. Its strong antiviral and germicidal properties are useful in repeated infections. Its fungicidal properties help clear vaginal thrush and are of value with genital infections generally. Tea tree alleviates urinary tract problems such as cystitis. It gives relief to genital and anal itching as well as general itching, from chicken pox to rashes caused by insect bites. It is said to give some protection against x-ray therapy in breast cancer. It will apparently reduce scarring when applied before treatment, as the protective film will guard against very deep penetration of the x-rays. This oil helps to ease otitis (inflammation of the ear) and reduces pus in infected wounds. It clears ports and blemishes caused by chicken pox and shingles. Tea tree is useful with burns, sores, sunburn, ringworm, warts, herpes and athlete's foot. It is helpful with dry conditions of the scalp as well as dandruff. This oil blends well with cinnamon, clove, cypress, eucalyptus, ginger, lavender and thyme. (Wharton, 2009.)

Thyme (Thymus vulgaris): Thyme has a rather sweet and strongly herbal fragrance. It is well known as being an antirheumatic, antiseptic, antispasmodic, aphrodisiac, cardiac tonic, cicatrizing, diuretic, emmenagogue, expectorant and insecticide. This is a very potent oil, one of the strongest antiseptics, with the possibility of high toxicity with prolonged use. It should not be used in cases of high blood pressure nor in pregnancy. Thyme activates brain cells, thereby aiding memory and concentration. It revives feelings of exhaustion and combats depression. It fortifies the lungs when treating colds, coughs and sore throats particularly tonsillitis and laryngitis. This oil is rather warming and helps to eliminate phlegm. It helps the body fight disease and raises low blood pressure. Since its stimulating effect facilitates the removal of uric acid it may be recommended for rheumatism, gout and arthritis. Thyme may stop nosebleeds. It helps with a sluggish digestion and wind. This oil speeds delivery in childbirth and expelling the afterbirth; therefore it could cause miscarriage. A tonic for the scalp, it is effective with dandruff and hair loss. This scent blends well with bergamot, cedarwood, chamomile and lemon. (Wharton, 2009.) ***Magickal uses and associations:*** Courage, conscious mind, health, Venus and Water. (Cunningham, 2004.)

Tolu Balsam (Myroxlon toluiferum): Tolu Balsam has a balsamic scent. Its scent is calming and grounding. This oil is an emollient and a skin conditioner. (Wharton, 2009.)

Valerian root (Valeriana officinalis): This oil is highly sedative in action. Due to its "dirty-socks" smell, it is not an oil for perfumery. [Author's note: I have found that when people need this oil, usually they are so stressed and very overtired that Valerian has a spicy scent. It is then that you know that they need this herb.] As a relaxing and sleep-inducing blend it has no equal. It is also known to calm down dogs and cats, although cats do tend to be more sensitive to essential oils than dogs. This oil should be used with caution on dogs and cats. (Wharton, 2009.)

Vanilla Extract (Vanilla plantifolia): Vanilla has a balsamic and sweet fragrance. It is good for anxiety, stress, anger, hypertension, emollient and works well as an aphrodisiac. This oil blends well with sandalwood and vetiver. (Wharton, 2009.) ***Magickal uses and associations:*** Physical energy, love, sex, magickal energy, Venus and Water. (Cunningham, 2004.)

Verbena (Lippia citriodora): Verbena smells of sweet lemons. It is an antiseptic, antispasmodic, aphrodisiac, digestive, emollient, insecticide and stomachic. Recent pharmacological tests have proven this oil to be phototoxic and a strong skin sensitizer. It is not recommended for massages. It is famous for banishing depression due to its tonic, soothing effect on the parasympathetic nervous system. Verbena works on the digestive system, especially controlling stomach spasms, cramps, nausea, indigestion and flatulence. It stimulates the appetite and has a cooling action on the liver as it mitigates inflammation, infection as in cirrhosis and could be beneficial in cases of alcoholism. This oil is helpful for bronchitis, soothes asthmatic coughs, as well as nasal and sinus congestion. It is said to avert convulsions. Verbena calms heart palpitations and may help with nervous insomnia. Its reputation as an aphrodisiac probably stems from its ability to calm underlying tension. Verbena oil keeps down skin puffiness. It blends well with basil, bergamot, chamomile, geranium, neroli, rose and rosemary. (Wharton, 2009.)

Vetivert (Vetiveria zizanoides): This oil has a deep, smoky and earthy aroma. It is an antiseptic, aphrodisiac, sedative and nervine. It is a calming oil, excellent for stress and tension, working by settling the nerves. It may be useful in helping people ease off tranquilizers. It is said to cleanse the aura and to strengthen the auric shield, which can be instrumental in keeping out disease. This oil is very helpful in cases of mental and physical exhaustion. It assists with increasing blood flow, thereby being able to alleviate muscular aches and pains. It is a tonic to the reproductive system, and its relaxing quality seems to have some effect on tension underlying sexual problems. It is helpful in cases of insomnia. Vetivert may have a healing effect on acne. This scent blends well with frankincense, geranium, grapefruit, jasmine, lavender, rose, sandalwood and ylang ylang. (Wharton, 2009.) *Magickal uses and associations:* Protection, money, Venus and Earth. (Cunningham, 2004.)

Wintergreen (Gaultheria procumbens): Wintergreen has a very refreshing aroma. Use with caution; this essential oil is approximately 99 percent salicylate, the main ingredient in aspirin (irritant, sensitizing). Use tiny amounts in muscle/joint blends and do a patch test for those with sensitive skin. Not recommended for usage in persons who take aspirin regularly. (Wharton, 2009.)

Yarrow (Achillea millifoleum): Its aroma is dry and herbaceous with a pale yellow to brilliant blue color. It's a well-known anti-inflammatory and is indicated for prostate or menstrual problems as well as neuralgia. Because of its high content of azulene, yarrow oil is used in skin care for acne, eczema and inflammation, to minimize varicose veins and reduce scars. Yarrow provides protection from ticks. It is also used to counter the ill effects of radiation therapy. (Wharton, 2009.) *Magickal uses and associations:* Psychic awareness, courage, love, Venus and Water. (Cunningham, 2004.)

Ylang-Ylang (Canagana odorata; all grades): Ylang-Ylang has a sweet, floral and heavy aroma. The grades, I, II, III and Complete, indicate from which part of the steam distillation process the oil was obtained, with grade I being of the highest quality. Complete is made up of all fractionations of the oil, and grade III is an excellent ingredient for soap-making. Ylang-Ylang Complete has a finer, more intense creamy-sweet fragrance. Ylang-Ylang both relaxes and arouses; in Europe therapists use it for sexual dysfunction. It is antidepressant, antiseptic, aphrodisiac and sedative. Excessive use may lead to headaches and nausea. Ylang-ylang could possibly irritate sensitive skins and is indicated against use on inflammatory skin conditions and dermatitis. This oil could well ease feelings of anger, anxiety, shock, panic and fear. Useful with rapid breathing and heartbeat, its sedative properties could help bring down high blood pressure. Ylang-ylang has a tonic and stimulating effect on the scalp, promoting a more luxurious hair growth. It blends well with bergamot, citronella, jasmine, lavender, lemon, rose, sandalwood and verbena. (Wharton, 2009.) ***Magickal uses and associations:*** Peace, love, sex, Venus and Water. (Cunningham, 2004.)

Precautions

- Avoid the following oils when pregnant: basil, cedarwood, clary sage, fennel, jasmine, juniper, lavender, marjoram, myrrh, rose, rosemary, sage and thyme.
- Avoid the following oils if you have epilepsy: camphor, fennel, hyssop, sage and rosemary.
- Always use 100 percent pure essential oils
- Do not use undiluted. If irritation occurs, consult a physician and put a few drops of carrier oils on location to absorb the essential oil.

Oils with other methods of healing

Essential oils go together with all different kinds of healing modalities. They can be used with crystal therapy: oils can be placed on the stones and then the stones can be placed on the body. For reflexology, oils can be diluted in a carrier oil for a refreshing foot or hand massage. Put some oil in a diffuser during a Reiki session to set the mood.

Zodiac oils

Capricorn: Rosemary (Wharton, 2009.), cypress, honeysuckle, lilac, mimosa, myrrh, patchouli, tonka, tulip, vertivert. (Cunningham, 2004.)

Aquarius: Frankincense (Wharton, 2009.), costmary, hops, lavender, lemon verbena, parsley, patchouli, pine, star anise, sweet pea. (Cunningham, 2004.)

Pisces: Bergamot (Wharton, 2009.), apple, camphor, cardamom, gardenia, hyacinth, jasmine, lily, mugwort, myrrh, palmarosa, sandalwood, vanilla, ylang-ylang. (Cunningham, 2004.)

Aries: Lavender (Wharton, 2009.), black pepper, clove, coriander, cumin, frankincense, ginger, neroli, pennyroyal, petitgrain, pine, woodruff. (Cunningham, 2004.)

Taurus: Patchouli (Wharton, 2009.), apple, cardamom, honeysuckle, lilac, magnolia, oakmoss, plumeria, rose, thyme, tonka, ylang-ylang. (Cunningham, 2004.)

Gemini: Chamomile (Wharton, 2009.), benzoin, bergamot mint, caraway, dill, lavender, lemongrass, lily of the valley, peppermint, sweet pea. (Cunningham, 2004.)

Cancer: Basil (Wharton, 2009.), chamomile, cardamom, jasmine, lemon, lily, myrrh, palmarosa, plumeria, rose, sandalwood, yarrow. (Cunningham, 2004.)

Leo: Vetivert (Wharton, 2009.), bay, basil, cinnamon, frankincense, ginger, juniper, lime, nasturtium, neroli, orange, petitgrain, rosemary. (Cunningham, 2004.)

Virgo: Rose (Wharton, 2009.), caraway, clary sage, costmary, cypress, dill, fennel, lemon balm, honeysuckle, oakmoss, patchouli. (Cunningham, 2004.)

Libra: Clary Sage (Wharton, 2009.), chamomile, daffodil, dill, eucalyptus, fennel, geranium, peppermint, pine, spearmint, palmarosa, vanilla. (Cunningham, 2004.)

Scorpio: Sandalwood, (Wharton, 2009.), black pepper, cardamom, coffee, galangal, hyacinth, hops, pennyroyal, pine, thyme, tuberose, woodruff. (Cunningham, 2004.)

Sagittarius: Juniper (Wharton, 2009.), bergamot, calendula, clove, hyssop, lemon balm, mace, nutmeg, oakmoss, rosemary, saffron. (Cunningham, 2004.)

MORE RECIPES

Fayre Canacea…
Well seene in everie science that mote be,
And everie secret worke of nature's ways.
In power of herbes
O who can tell
The hidden power of herbes
And might of magic spell
—Edmund Spenser, *The Faerie Queen*
in Juliette de Bairacli Levy, *Traveler's Joy*, 1994.

INSECT REPELLENT OIL

This is also an excellent remedy for bites, burns, wounds and chilblains. In a blender or grinder, powder dried southernwood, mugwort, dragonweed (tarragon), or wormwood (these are all artemisias). Rosemary, rue, thyme and basil may be added. If using fresh herbs, twice as much must be added as the dried, and they must be chopped very finely. Use a cupful of a light oil like sunflower or corn oil and a teaspoon of any kind of vinegar (except malt vinegar) to every two large spoonfuls of the mixed, chopped herbs. Place in a jar and stand it in a container of sand, which holds the heat, in strong sunlight. Shake well every day. After five days, strain off the old herbs, pressing them to get the oil out. Put in the same amount of new herbs, discarding the old ones. Do this at least three times, leaving the herbs in the last batch for five days up to two weeks. Do not put this oil directly on the skin: moisten a cotton ball, apply some of the oil to it, then apply it to the skin. (Levy, 1997.)

Relaxing and calming oil combos Mix all combos with 1–2 tablespoons carrier oil. (Wharton, 2009)	
Spearmint 3 drops Eucalyptus 2 drops	Cedarwood 3 drops Sage 2 drops
Lavender 3 drops Palmarosa 2 drops	Lavender 3 drops Vanilla 3 drops
Bay 2 drops Rose 2 drops	Lemongrass 3 drops Orange 1 drop
Geranium 2 drops Cedarwood 3 drops	Rosewood 3 drops Geranium 3 drops
Stimulating and uplifting oil combos	
Grapefruit 3 drops Peppermint 2 drops	Orange 3 drops Ginger 3 drops
Bergamot 3 drops Lavender 3 drops	Tea tree 3 drops Eucalyptus 2 drops
Orange 3 drops Patchouli 2 drops	Peppermint 2 drops Lavender 3 drops
Rosemary 2 drops Lime 4 drops	Rosewood 3 drops Orange 2 drops

Other crafts using aromatherapy

Sachets and Potpourri—You can use dried herbs and flowers in combination with essential oils to make potpourri and sachets. To do this, place the dried herb of your choice in a brown paper bag with a few drops of essential oil(s). Shake well or blend with your hands, close the bag and leave over night. This mixture can be put in a bowl or a sachet bag. To refresh, put the mixture back in a bag and shake well; this releases the oils once again for a fresh scent. (Wharton, 2009.)

Another way to make potpourri is to collect as many scented flowers as possible, such as roses, acacia, violets, pinks, lily of the valley, lilacs, orange or lemon blossoms, mignonette, heliotrope, narcissi, jonquils, (small amounts of) blossoms from lemon balm, rosemary, thyme and myrtle. Spread these blossoms out to dry. When they are fully dry, put them in a tall glass jar, layering a mixture of two parts coarse salt to one part powdered orris root. When the jar is filled, seal the jar and let it sit for one month. After a month, add rose water to moisten the mixture until it reaches the lowest layers. This mixture can be put in cotton bags as sachets and can also scent writing paper. (Levy, 1997.)

Aromatherapy candles—Melt wax down, preferably beeswax or soy wax; let it cool a bit and add oils. Remember to let the wax cool or it will evaporate the oil. Pour into molds, add a wick and let cool. (Wharton, 2009.)

Lip balms and glosses—Combine some cocoa butter, sweet almond oil and a few drops of your favorite oil for glosses, and add a little beeswax for balms. Cocoa mint lip balm: 1½ ounce cocoa butter, 1 ounce beeswax, 1½ ounce shea butter, 2 capsules vitamin E, 10–15 drops peppermint oil. Put in tubes or containers. (Wharton, 2009.)

Bath salts—1½ cups Epsom salts, 1 cup baking soda, ½ cup salt, some drops of oils until the scent is appealing to you. Another mixture is just sea salt and oil. (Wharton, 2009.)

Bath bombs—1–2 parts Epsom salts, 2 parts baking soda, 1 part cornstarch, 1–2 parts citric acid, 1 part grapeseed oil. Knead until dough-like (not sticky). Add drops of oil until you like the scent. Roll into balls and wrap in cellophane until ready to use. (Wharton, 2009.)

Magickal oils

Oils can be made according to seasonal, lunar phase and astrological phases. They can be charged with Reiki or a specific intention. When making your oil you can chant over the oil, holding your hands over it sending a direct flow of energy into the oil. (Malbrough, 2003.) Silver Ravenwolf recommends recharging your oils every month to six months to keep them energized. (Ravenwolf, 2006.) Crystal chips can be put into the container to charge the oil with a specific intention; for instance, an amethyst chip in an oil for peace or a rose quartz chip in an oil for love would add extra energy to your oil. A piece of root, herb or lodestone can be added to a finished oil. Magickal oils can be used for anointing people, candles or tools. (Malbrough, 2003.)

BLESSING OIL

2 parts frankincense   1 part benzoin gum

Add 2 tablespoons of this mixture to 2 ounces of base oil. (Malbrough, 2003.)

HEALING OIL

⅛ cup base oil   7 drops niaouli

4 drops eucalyptus   2 drops pine (Cunningham, 2004.)

HEALTH ATTRACTING OIL

2 tablespoons of any of the following herbs in 2 ounces of oil:

Rose   Carnation

Gardenia   Grated lemon peel

Lemon flowers (Malbrough, 2003.)

PROTECTION OIL

Mix equal parts of the following: Sandalwood

Patchouli leaves   Gardenia petals

Use 2 tablespoons to 2 ounces of oil. Add a pinch of salt to bottle.

This should be worn as a perfume; anoint the forehead, throat and breast bone. (Malbrough, 2003.)

NINE MYSTERIES OIL

Orange   Violet

Wintergreen

This oil is used for overcoming all business and domestic troubles, as well as blessing a home or business. This can be used to sprinkle around the room, dress a candle or mixed as an incense and burned. (Slater, 2005.)

SABBAT INCENSE OR OIL

1 drop benzoin oil

Equal parts: patchouli	Sandalwood
Orris	Rose
Fennel	Thyme
Rue	Chamomile
Pennyroyal	Vervain (Slater, 2005.)

TRINITY OIL

Hyssop	Olive oil
Verbena	

This oil brings blessings to you in every area of your life, including spiritual and material endeavors. (Slater, 2005.)

WOOD SONG

Violet	Honeysuckle
Mint (Slater, 2005.)	

HOLY OIL

Olive oil base	Lily oil
Rose oil	Cross in the bottle

This is an oil used for blessing candles before a ritual. (Slater, 2005.)

Notes—Aromatherapy

Cunningham, S. *Magical Aromatherapy: The Power of Scent.* St. Paul: Llewellyn Publications, 2004.

Holy Bible Revised Standard Version, Book of Song of Solomon. Chicago: International Council of Religious Education, 1928.

Levy, J. *Traveler's Joy.* Woodstock: Ash Tree Publishing, 1994.

Levy, J. *Common Herbs for Natural Health.* Woodstock: Ash Tree Publishing, 1997.

Levy, J. *Nature's Children.* Woodstock: Ash Tree Publishing, 1997.

Malbrough, R. *Charms, Spells and Formulas.* St. Paul: Llewellyn Publications, 2003.

Moura, A. *Green Witchcraft II: Balancing Light and Shadow.* St. Paul: Llewellyn Publications, 2007.

Ravenwolf, S. *Mindlight: Secrets of Energy, Magick & Manifestation.* St. Paul: Llewellyn Publications, 2006.

Riggs, M. *The Scented Woman: Create Your Own Signature Perfume From Essential Oils.* New York: Viking Penguin, 1992.

Schiller, D. and Schiller, C. *500 Formulas for Aromatherapy: Mixing Essential Oils for Every Use.* New York: Sterling Publishing Company, 1994.

Slater, H. *Magickal Formulary Spellbook. Book I.* New York: Magickal Childe, Inc,, 2005.

Wharton, L. *Pixie Hollow Institute Aromatherapy Course Manual.* East Greenville: Pixie Hollow Institute, 2009.

Worwood, V. *The Complete Book of Essential Oils and Aromatherapy: Over 600 Natural, Non-Toxic and Fragrant Recipes to Create Health–Beauty–a Safe Home Environment.* Novato: New World Library, 1991.

Worwood, V. *The Fragrant Mind: Aromatherapy for Personality, Mind, Mood and Emotion.* Novato: New World Library, 1996.

Worwood, V. *The Fragrant Heavens.* New York: Bantam Books, 1999.

www.haikupoetshut.com/basho1.html

CHAPTER 8

The Moon, The Days,
The Seasons, and The Elements

Hail to Thee, O Jewel of the Night
Hail to Thee, O Lady of the Heavens
Hail to Thee, O Jewel of the Night
Hail to Thee, O Queen of the Stars
Hail to Thee, O Jewel of the Night
Hail to Thee, O Mother of the Worlds
—Lisa Thiel, "Jewel of the Night,"
archaic prayer honoring the moon, 1997.

Wise Woman Craft follows and honors the moons as well as the seasons. I ask my students to track how they feel during each moon phase and season. One's energy level, mood, dream activity, and any other noticeable changes should be recorded in the student's journal. While this concept may be new to some, it is in reality quite old. The earliest myths are of stories in a matriarchal society where worship of the moon dominated, led by priestesses. Remember that Jewish, Islamic, and Christian holidays are based on the moon's phases. Hannibal's treaty with the Gauls was interpreted by a court of Gallic Matrons, revered old wise women who decided on disputes. We can even see this in the word, "matrimony," which reminds us that there was a time when matrilineal ties were adhered to and illegitimacy of children was not a concept. Matriarchal societies were more peaceful as evidenced by a lack of weapons found on archeological sites of cultures ruled by women. "[What] the myths of the moon…have in common is the taint of centuries of patriarchal revision. It is possible to read them as stories of the times of matriarchal-patriarchal struggle and after the firm establishment of patriarchy. It is equally crucial for us to open our collective memories in order to imagine what each story was when another mode dominated the Earth's cultures and we lived our lives coherent with our deepest psyches." (Rush, 1976.)

MOON PHASES

The moon affects the tides, as well as the ebb and flow of the water on Earth, utilizing gravitational pull. The human body is over 70 percent water so people are very affected by the moon phases and the pull she has on us. The term "lunacy" came about because people noticed the strange behaviors of some people during the full moon. The aerial parts of herbs (the parts above the ground) are more potent during the waxing and full moon. This is why when you buy a farmers' almanac the moon phases are included. Farmers found that seeds planted during the waxing moon were stronger, as were animals born during this phase. Fishermen had more success with fishing, crabbing, shrimping and clamming during this period. Removal of horns or castration was done during the waning moon because there was less bleeding. (Bowes, 1999.)

Ancient people used the moon to measure time. The Sanskrit root "me" means "measure" and both the words moon as well as month were derived from this term. Women bled together according to the moon phases. The ancient Celtic calendars are based on thirteen lunar months. The Earth is orbited by the moon every twenty-nine and a half days, but the sun signs are about a day longer than the lunar month. This makes each new moon start earlier in a sun-sign period, until a new moon occurs so soon after the start of the sun sign that there is room for the entire lunar month before the sun sign changes. Two new moons often occur during the summer instead of the winter because the sun signs in the summer are a little longer. The moon for the thirteenth month is called the Blue Moon or Fairy Moon and is said to hold much power. The Jewish, Hindu, and Chinese calendars have an extra month during the year. The full moons in Taurus and Gemini are believed to be the moons that open the door to higher consciousness in Buddhism. The thirteenth moon is associated with Arachne, the spider, who spins the web of life because she is said to have fallen between Gemini and Taurus. (Bowes, 1999.)

The new moon is a time of beginnings and planting seeds. It is a time to honor new endeavors and journeys, whether they are inward or outward. The energy for the new moon is the maiden and spring. The waxing moon is the growing moon and it is a time for increase in a life, whether it be prosperity, health, peace, wisdom, or love and friendship.

The full moon is the pinnacle; its energies last three days before and three days after the moon. The gravitational pull of both sun and moon, with the earth in middle, sets up these extremes. Whatever sun sign the full moon is in has a strong effect on our energies. The full moon is also associated with fertilization and ovulation; its energy is associated with the mother as well as summer. This energy is more like the pregnant mother, swollen with possibilities. She is the Feminine Divine. This is a time for sending out requests including creating healing potions for ourselves or our loved ones. This is a time to cleanse, charge and dedicate our crystals as well as our tools. When you feel empty or in need of guidance, go out in the full moon to be refilled with joy, power and healing. Light a candle, write out your dreams, goals and requests, knowing in your heart you have been heard. The full moon is associated with the fairies as well as the fulfillment of wishes as expressed in Doreen Valiente's *Charge of the Goddess*: "Listen to the words of the Great Mother, Who of old was called Artemis, Astarte, Dionne, Melusine, Aphrodite, Cerridwen, Diana, Arianrhod, Brigid, and by many other names. Whenever you have need of anything, once a month, and better it be when the moon is full, you shall assemble in some secret place and adore the spirit of Me Who is Queen of all the Wise." (Valiente, 2000.)

The waning moon is a time of clearing away, harvesting the roots of vegetables and herbs, weeding as well as banishing. If you wish to release things in your life, now is the time. This is a time to start a diet or work on stopping a bad habit. The waning moon is associated with the crone and autumn. Three days before the new moon there is the dark of the moon. This is a time of releasing or strong banishment. One might find that they feel depressed or have a low amount of energy. If for instance, as a healer, you wanted to work on shrinking a tumor on a client, the waning moon and dark moon would be powerful times to strengthen your intentions. This is the time to make a poke root tincture to fight breast cancer.

The Seasons

The Wheel of the Year brings different activities in nature. A wise woman who lives close to the Earth changes with the Seasons. Her activities in the home and the garden change too. Spring is the time of the maiden; the energies of the maiden goddesses such as Kore and Artemis are honored. This is a time to plant seeds, clear out our gardening beds and start new projects. The renewal of the Earth is a reminder of the renewal we experience also. In ancient times people celebrated the Spring because it meant not only was there more food for their families, but they had survived the winter. We go to grocery stores; we are disconnected from the Earth's energies. That is why it is important to reconnect with the moon's phases and seasonal energies by journaling how we feel as well as paying attention to Nature.

The summer is the time of the mother, the energies of goddesses such as Isis, Hera, and Demeter or Mother Mary. It is a time of growth and plenty. The fall is a time of harvest and year's end. The ancient peoples preserved their food, and made their meads, ales, and wines. This was when they got ready for the winter. The winter is a time of the crone, goddesses such as Hecate and Mother Holle. This is the time nature rests and it is the time we are supposed to rest also.

Below is a description of the Wheel of the Year, the holidays, and their dates. It is believed by some that ancient agricultural societies did not follow this calendar, that they only honored the four quarter days. The Cleansing Tide falls between Yule and the Spring Equinox; this is a time to discard things that no longer are of use to you. The Growing Tide comes between March and June, after you have weeded and cleansed in the previous months. This is a time of new ideas, progress and success. The Reaping Tide is from Midsummer to the Autumnal Equinox; this is when plans, skills and abilities pay off. Resting Tide is from September to Yule and its name implies its energy: just as Mother Nature now rests, so should you. (Green, 1995.)

Samhain (SAH-wen or SOW-en) or Halloween is considered the time when the veil is thin. This means that we can contact those who have crossed over. It is a time to honor those who have passed; it is a very old celebration. (Madden and Roberts, 2006.) The dates for this greater Sabbat are October 31–November 2. Samhain is considered one of the quarter days of the sun sabbats which are based on the astronomical position of the sun. It is a celebration of the new year and a feast of the end of the harvest. This is the third and last harvest. The word Samhain is an Irish Gaelic word that may means "the summer's end" or "one together," reflecting the time of the veil being thin. The Crone rules this period when her son and lover dies. This is a time when you can place pictures of the loved ones who have passed on your altar. People sometimes do past life work during this period. (McCoy, 1998.)

Yule or Midwinter is the birth of the Solstice Sun; the rebirth of the Great God. This day is the shortest day of the year and it is the time the Child of Light returns to bringer longer days. Winter Solstice is considered one of the oldest Sabbats, perhaps 12,000 to 20,000 years old.

(McCoy, 1998.) The traditions of bringing in greenery, caroling, wassailing and decorating a tree all come from the original holiday of Yule. (Madden and Roberts, 2006.) Early Christians wanted to convert people so they made this time Jesus's birth. The reality is that when Jesus was born, the lambs were already in the field making his birth in the spring, not winter. This makes sense because he was called the Lamb of God. The date of this holiday falls between December 19 and 23.

Imbolc, Candlemas, Imbolg or St. Brigid's Day, is considered one of the four fire festivals. This holiday falls halfway between the Winter Solstice and the Spring Equinox. Imbolc is one of the quarter days because it falls between February 1 and 3. Candlemas has the energy of birth and new beginnings. (Madden and Roberts, 2006.) This is the traditional time when the Greenfire women put out their Bridie's blankets. These are cloths or blankets put outside sometime between January 31 and February 3 to be blessed by Bridget's healing properties. The blankets are used to lay over friends, family, and clients during healings. This holiday was originally associated with the Irish tri-fold Goddess Brigid. The early Christians had a lot of difficulty getting the Irish to give her up so they made her Saint Brigid,; the midwife for Mother Mary. When she was a Goddess her flame was guarded by 19 priestesses, each guarding it for one day, and on the twentieth day she guarded it herself. Then she became Mary's midwife, so she was guarded by 19 nuns, and on the twentieth day St. Brigid guarded the flame herself.

This time period is associated with festivals of women's mysteries and ritual practices reserved for women only. Imbolc may have this reference to women's rites due to her followers becoming nuns to continue to guard her flame in her shrine in Kildare. Up until the early twentieth century, young women in Irish villages would dress themselves in old clothing as St. Brighid, carrying her image through the streets. These girls would beg for alms for "poor Biddy," Brighid's nickname. This was thought to bring luck and a good harvest. Lighting candles or a bonfire and divining are good practices at this time. Some people like to make a Bridie bed, making a straw doll and dressing her as a bride. (McCoy, 1998.)

Ostara, or the Vernal Equinox, comes from the Old English Eostre and Old High German which are the names of a putative Germanic goddess whose Anglo-Saxon month, Eostur-monath, has given its name to the Christian festival of Easter. Eostre is a Teutonic Goddess of spring and fertility. (McCoy, 1998.) Ostara's dates fall between March 20 and 23. It is an equinox, which means "equal night." After the equinox the days will start to be longer and the sunlight stronger. This Sabbat celebrates balance and life renewed, but it was not a

Sabbat for the Old Celts until the Saxons brought it to their attention around CE 600. Ostara is symbolized by the egg. It is interesting that balance and eggs are associated with this holiday because you can balance an egg at the exact time of the equinox. This is a time to find balance within ourselves and our world. (Madden and Roberts, 2006.)

Beltaine, Bealtaine, or May Day on May 1 is the second of spring festivals. The name of this Sabbat means "good fire" or "Bel's fire" in honor of the Celtic Sun god Bel. In ancient Ireland, cattle were passed between two fires to protect and bless them with fertility. Couples would jump over or pass between fires to also increase their chances of having children. This is the time of the Great Marriage between the Goddess and the God. May Eve is also considered very important and it is the time you can hear fairy music. (Madden and Roberts, 2006.)

Beltaine is associated with handfastings (marriages) in modern times. In ancient Ireland it was a time of divorce, with marriages occurring in November. In Scotland every village would light its own "need fire" or "tein-eigin," a continually burning small fire that was kept burning for home or cooking. This was time of dancing around maypoles, with white and red, symbolizing the maiden becoming the mother or the Goddess and the God. (McCoy, 1998.)

Midsummer, Summer Solstice, Mother night or Litha, is said to be sacred to fairies. It falls between June 19 and 23. (Madden and Roberts, 2006.) This is when the sun is at its peak. This is also called St. John's Day and is the traditional day associated with harvesting St. John's wort. Among feminist herbalists, St. John's wort is called St. Joan's wort because this herb makes a wonderful suntan lotion and St. Joan knew more about burning than St. John. (Weed, 1985.) June 25, a time close to the Midsummer, is the Feast of Aine, an Irish fire and cattle Goddess, who some say lost her day to St. John. It was once a tradition, up until the early twentieth century, to wave a torch over the growing fields for protection and fertility. Midsummer Eve processions by torchlight in her town of Munster were a common custom. (McCoy, 1998.)

Luhnasadh, Lammas or Loaf Mass, is the first of three harvest festivals and named after the God Lugh; the term meaning "Lugh's wedding." This Sabbat falls on August 1 or 2. It is a traditional time for the Scots games where there is much piping, dancing, caber tossing and sheepdog trials. (McCoy, 1998.)

Mabon, Harvest Home, Alban Elfed, Second Harvest or Autumnal Equinox, falls between September 19 and 23. This is the start of the fall season. Divination, shadow work, protection and prosperity are activities for this time of year. (Madden and Roberts, 2006.) The name Mabon is believed to be the name of the Welsh God "Young Son." In Irish customs blackberries, which are sacred to Brighid, must be harvested between now and Samhain, the leftover going to the pookas, the fairies who claim unharvested foods. This is the time the Goddess enters cronehood; it is a time to decorate graves with symbols of rebirth. Mabon is another equinox, but the dark is more dominant. (McCoy, 1998.)

Altars

To some, depending on your religious and spiritual backgrounds, having a personal or family altar might seem strange. An altar may be already set up in your home, and you might not think of it as an altar, but it is a sacred area. It could be a spot where there are things special to you or photos of loved ones no longer with you. This is an altar. It is a place where you rest your eyes to get a feeling of peace. Altars often celebrate the season, remember loved ones who have crossed over or celebrate family and friends. Changing the decoration of the dining room table to celebrate the seasons is a subtle way to make sacred space. If there is an issue you are working on such as health, you can have a photo of the person happy and healthy. The idea is to focus on the positive outcome. (Streep, 1997.)

In her book, *Altars Made Easy: A Complete Guide To Creating Your Own Sacred Space,* Peg Streep describes what altars mean to each person. "When men and women talk about their altars, regardless of their faith or rituals, the same words come up in their descriptions. Some of them refer to the process of seeking the self: energy, direction, meaning. Still others address state of mind: peacefulness, calm, strength. Usually, too, there are words that connect to finding the sacred in daily life, focusing on something larger than the self and the day-to-day: prayer, meditation, communication. It becomes immediately clear that making an altar is not like decorating; it is a search for meaning or a process of discovering what has meaning for you." (Streep, 1997.)

When my students start to study with me, I ask them to look around their home and work space. I ask them to look for altars they may already have and acknowledge them for what they are, a sacred place that helps to incorporate the Divine into the mundane. One of my suggestions to my students is to consider making a special spot that is sacred to them in the home where they can light a candle and refocus. Many of them already have an altar, but for others it is a completely new idea.

THE DAYS OF THE WEEK

Day of the Week	Associations
Monday	Moon, inner visions, divination, finding water and illnesses, intuition
Tuesday	Mars, energy, enthusiasm, strength, number 5
Wednesday	Mercury, travel, communication, color orange, finding lost friends
Thursday	Jupiter, number 4, color royal blue, monetary success, planning.
Friday	Venus, color green, number seven, Nature, healing, love, partnerships
Saturday	Saturn, banishing, number 3, incense myrrh, metal lead, wisdom
Sunday	Sun, healing, color gold or yellow, knowledge (Green, 1995.)

ELEMENTS

Element	Associations
Earth	Gnomes, guardians of the North, Winter, green, physical world, abundance, fertility, wisdom, prosperity
Air	Sylph, guardians of the East, Spring, yellow, intellect, illumination, clear thinking, new beginnings, creation
Fire	Salamanders, guardians of the South, Summer, red, inner child, inspiration, passion, creativity, change
Water	Undines, guardians of the West, Autumn, blue, setting sun, place of dreams, death, inner visions, journeys, emotions

By understanding the energies of the moon, the seasons, the days, and their elements, one can see how they affect individuals. This can also help a person when doing a healing or a ritual utilizing the energies of each while incorporating the elements.

PAY ATTENTION

It is said that the land will provide you with what you need. My father went further than that and said that for every poison, there was an antidote nearby. Waverly Fitzgerald challenges her students to see what is in bloom in each season and what is growing in the wild. She asks us to identify plants that grow around us and learn about the type of land we live on.

Some believe that it is the fey that give us gifts in the wild, whether they be volunteer plants or feathers, so it is important to say thank you. My husband used to suffer from asthma; no matter where he moved, mullein would volunteer in his garden. I never saw mullein until we were married and she offered herself up to us. If we acknowledge that we are part of the Universal Life Force, then it should not be surprising when plants appear that we need. Your gifts should be recorded in your journal.

Notes—The Moon, The Days, The Seasons, and The Elements

Bowes, S. *Life Magic: The Power of Positive Witchcraft.* New York: Simon & Schuster Editions, 1999.

Green, M. *A Witch Alone.* London: Thorsons, 1995.

Madden, K. and Roberts, L. *Magickal Crafts.* Franklin Lakes: The Career Press, Inc., 2006.

McCoy, E. *Celtic Women's Spirituality: Accessing the Cauldron of Life.* St. Paul: Llewellyn Publications, 1998.

Rush, A. *Moon, Moon.* New York: Random House, 1976.

Streep, P. *Altars Made Easy: A Complete Guide To Creating Your Own Sacred Space.* New York: Harper Collins Publishers, 1997.

Thiel, L. *"Jewel of the Night (Chant)"* in *Invocation of the Graces.* Sacred Dream Records, 1997.

Valiente, D. *Charge of the Goddess: The Mother of Modern Witchcraft.* London: Hexagon Publications, 2000.

Weed, S. *Wise Woman Herbal for the Childbearing Year.* Woodstock: Ash Tree Publishing, 1985.

CHAPTER 9

THE FEMININE DIVINE AND OUR FOREMOTHERS

When, however, one reads of a witch being ducked, of a woman possessed by devils, of a wise woman selling herbs, or even a very remarkable man who had a mother, then I think we are on the track of a lost novelist, a suppressed poet . . . indeed, I would venture to guess that Anon, who wrote so many poems without signing them, was often a woman.

—Virginia Woolf, 1928.

THE FEMININE DIVINE

A good wife who can find? She is far more precious than jewels. The heart of her husband trusts in her, and he will have no lack of gain. She does him good, and not harm, all the days of her life. She seeks wool and flax, and works with willing hands. She is like the ships of the merchant; she brings her food from afar. She rises while it is yet night and provides food for her household and tasks for her maidens. She considers a field and buys it: with the fruit of her hands she plants a vineyard. She girds her loins with strength and makes her arms strong. She perceives that her merchandise is profitable. Her lamp does not go out at night.

She puts her hands to the distaff, and her hands hold the spindle. She opens her hands to the poor, and reaches out her hands to the needy. She is not afraid of snow for her household, for all her household are clothed in scarlet.

She makes herself coverings; her clothing is fine linen and purple. Her husband is known in the gates, when he sits among the elders of the land. She makes linen garments and sells them; she delivers girdles to the merchant. Strength and dignity are her clothing and she laughs at the time to come. She opens her mouth with wisdom, and the teaching of kindness is on her tongue. She looks well to the ways of her household, and does not eat the bread of idleness. Her children rise up and call her blessed; her husband also, and he praises her.

—Proverbs 31: 10–28.

For many women one of the greatest challenges when studying Wise Woman Craft is finding the Feminine Divine and positive female role models. Many women feel betrayed by their religions, their family upbringing, their society or their understanding of history. One of the requirements of their study is to find the Feminine Divine within their own spiritual path. Some women are Catholic and already work with Mary or a particular female saint. Others are pagan and already have a deity they work with. But for many women the challenge is difficult and frightening. They have been convinced by patriarchal societies that the Feminine Divine does not exist and to say she does will send them to Hell.

I was raised a Born-Again Christian, so for my healing, I needed to find the Feminine Divine within my own religion and culture. I always felt that the Goddess ended up "on the cutting room floor" as she would during a movie's editing. During my studies with the White Moon School I was required to study goddesses and exceptional women. I have included my work on the Shekenah and St. Hildegard of Bingen.

THE SHEKENAH

This is the time when thanks are given for the fertility of the fields. It was traditional in the Scottish Highlands to sprinkle drops of menstrual blood on doorposts and around the house using a wisp of straw and on Lammas Day people smeared their floors and cows with menstrual blood, an act of especial protective power at Lammas and at Beltane. Lammas is the Festival of First Fruits. Fig trees in the Holy Land also produce their first fruit about this time and up to late September.

—André Zsigmond, "Mythology, Menstruation and the 'Woman with the Issue of Blood,'" *The Goddess Within*, 2009.

The Shekenah is the Hebrew Goddess that is invited into Jewish homes during the Sabbath. One of the first appearances of the Shekenah is in Exodus. When the Israelites set out from Succoth in their escape from Egypt, the Shekenah appeared as a cloudy pillar in the day and a fiery pillar by night. (Exodus 13:20.) She was present at the crossing of the Red Sea and stayed with the Israelites for the forty years they were in the desert. The Goddess appears in the Zohar, Book of Splendor, and it is said that Rachel was the embodiment of the Shekenah as perceived by Jacob, who met her at the well, the same well where Rebekah was told of her marriage to Isaac, Hagar was told of her son's future, and Zipporah was told of her union with Moses. The root of her name, *Shaken,* means dwelling or to abide. Her name is also associated with the word *Sekeen* which means knife, giving some scholars reason to believe that she is associated with circumcision. The next part of her name, *Ken,* means Cosmic Power. She is considered the feminine element of divinity and the equivalent of Shakti, for she is a life force and a catalyst of change. When the prophet Samuel anointed Saul for service to God, he was instructed to go to Rachel's tomb first. She died on a journey by herself, so she can guide others in honoring the natural cycles of change. (Kelly, 2003.)

The Goddess is called "the Spring of Gardens and the Well of Living Waters." One of her symbols is the house or womb, for within her resides primal wisdom, making one of her names *Sophia*. Her name, *Hokhma* or Wisdom, gives her an important role with the early Christian Gnostics as the "World Soul." It is said that King Solomon "married" her for "to set all one's thoughts on Her is true Wisdom and to be ever aware of Her is the sure way to perfect Peace." (Wisdom of Solomon, about 50 BCE.) The Goddess is also identified with the Holy Apple Tree. She is considered The Tree of Life. The Shekenah is the Divine's embodiment of wisdom, nature and folly. She represents folly because she is influenced by her people, her worshipers, and if they do wrong, she leaves. (Kelly, 2003.)

The Shekenah resided in the Ark of the Covenant, Mount Sinai and the Mount of Olives. She appeared to Noah and Moses. It is believed that it was the Shekenah that took Moses out of the Nile, not Pharaoh's daughter. The Shekenah and the Sophia are the two H's in the abbreviated name of God, YHVH. Y is God the Father, H is God the Mother, V is the Divine Son, H is the Divine Daughter. In Genesis God says, "Let *us* make man after our own image," leading many Jewish mystics and scholars of the Kabala to believe that Yahweh is talking to his wife. Some researchers believe that *she* is speaking to *him*. The Hebrew word for God in Genesis is Elohim, the plural of Eloah, a feminine title for the Goddess. Eloah or Elat is the female half of El. Based on this translation, the first being created by the Divine was a physical embodiment of the Divine, not male or female, a living Yin-Yang, so to speak. The lesser animals were split into male and female, but not the human. This is because Adam, whose name translated from Dam and Adamah in Hebrew means "blood" and "Earth," was a whole being. When Adam said he/she wanted a companion the female part of Adam was separated from the male. At this point male and female were still considered equals. (Kelly, 2003.)

The union of the Divine to create a being in their own image shows us that this God is a sexual God, leading some to believe that the Lord and Lady, channeled as one of the original forms of the Divine Masculine and Feminine would create a ceremony of Divine worship. The six-sided Star of David—two triangles represent the union of the Jehovah with his Shekenah— is described in the Song of Songs in the Bible. During some Jewish weddings the groom addresses his bride as, "My sister, my friend, my lover, my wife," and the bride says, "My brother, my friend, my lover, my husband." This ritual is based on Song of Songs and the meaning of YHVH as a combination of both masculine and feminine Divine. It is believed that during the ceremony the bride and groom are the embodiment of Jehovah and Shekenah. That is why they say when you are ill, have the bride say a prayer for your health prior to her getting married, and it will be answered. (Kelly, 2003.)

This Goddess is considered to be the tenth Sephirah and the moon. In the traditions of Judaism "blessing the moon" is a prayer of gratitude on the eve of every new moon. The Talmud says, "One who blesses the moon in the proper time is like one who is received by the Shekenah." (Sanhedrin 42a.) The Aramaic translation of the Lord's Prayer by Neil Douglas-Klotz shows evidence of the Goddess in Jesus's prayer, "Oh Birther, Mother-Father of the Cosmos, Hallowed be thy Name…" (Kelly, 2003.)

The Shekenah is also considered to be the Holy Spirit. Some believe that the Shekenah was the force, wind, or breath (Ruah) that blew across the Israelites to motivate them to leave Egypt. It enabled them to have the strength to leave the only home they ever knew. One of the translations of Shekenah is "Cosmic Living Breath." The Goddess is also known as "Holy" and "All Powerful," ascending and descending, often winged, and God's "light and glory." Being winged, her other symbol, the dove, appears in Jesus's baptism and to Noah in search of land. The Ruah descended on Miriam in the desert for seven days, making her a crone when she was permitted by the Divine to leave the cloud. Rabbi Shoni Labowitz believes this was so Miriam could help Moses's wife face menopause. (Kelly, 2003.)

She appears in Genesis as "the Breath of Life" that was breathed into Adam when he was created. It was the Holy Spirit that descended upon Mary when she was to conceive Jesus, making some believe that she was the embodiment of the Divine Mother, and suggesting that the Holy Trinity could be God the Mother (Mary or Sophia), God the Daughter (Mary Magdalene) and Goddess the Spirit Presence. The Holy Spirit's gifts are wisdom, strength, piety, counsel, love, joy, peace, kindness, mildness, control, speaking with wisdom, speaking in tongues, interpreting tongues, healing, miracles and prophecy. (Kelly, 2003.)

The Bible says, "Bless the Sabbath and keep it Holy." (Exodus 20:11.) She is known as the Sabbath Bride and the Sabbath Queen. It is for this reason that she is invited in by the woman of the house during the Jewish Sabbath. The woman faces west, lights the candles, waves her hands above the flames to invite the Shekenah, and then covers her face with her hands to finish the prayer. There are always two candles and two loaves of bread representing the duality of the Divine. Usually the bread is braided; some say that represents the Goddess's braids. Judith Berger describes how Jewish couples are encouraged to make love to conceive a child during the Sabbath because this child will be truly blessed. (Kelly, 2003.)

Rabbi Shoni Labowitz points out how the Asherah and the Shekenah overlap. She describes the Babylonian word for menstruation as *sabattu* which is a derivation of "sa-bat" meaning "heart rest." This was when the moon was the fullest, neither waxing nor waning. It was believed to be the time when the Goddess Asherah menstruated and is the forerunner of the Jewish Sabbath. Deuteronomy 12:23 says "the blood is the soul." In the Song of Songs or Song of Psalms, the Goddess says, "I will lead you into my mother's house, and she will teach me how to let you drink of the fragrant wine of my pomegranate." Here in this context the pomegranate represented menstruation. (Kelly, 2003.)

When Rachel took her household teraphim, which would have originally been her mother's, and sat on them to hide them from her father, saying she was bleeding, she was protecting her legacy, a celebration of a bleeding goddess. For these represent Rachel's heritage, the bleeding Goddess and the sabattu. Shoni tells us that the root letters for teraphim mean to heal, make whole, restore and cure. Rachel, the physical form of the Shekenah, has come to be the guardian of women's independence and heritage. Labowitz goes on to describe the importance of the sabbath candles, passed down from mother to daughter representing the matriarchal lineage. It also helped her to understand why no matter what was left behind when a Jewish family left their home, the mother always took the sabbath candles. (Kelly, 2003.)

Shekenah ritual

This can be done during the full or new moon or on the traditional Jewish Sabbath, Friday, eighteen minutes before sundown.

Supplies: Two yellow or orange candles, preferably the memorial candles in the thick glass, two loaves of braided Challah bread, orange- or citrus-scented incense, a small bowl or glass of cloves, bay leaves and/or cinnamon, a string or cord to make a hanger for prayer flags and five squares of different colored cloths, a paint pen or permanent marker, craft glue or a needle and thread to close the fold on the prayer flag over the cord.

The altar should be facing west so while you are working you are facing in that direction. It can have symbols of wisdom and wind as well as menstruation, such as an owl, a feather and a pomegranate. If you are doing this inside, try to open a door or window to invite the Goddess in.

Cast your circle and call the quarters or angels. I choose to call the angels for this: Raphael for East, Michael in the South, Gabriel for West, and Auriel in the North.

Facing west, light your incense, ground and center.

Sabbath queen blessings: "Blessed Mother, Sacred Flame, Holy Ruah, guide our aim."

Light your candles, cover your eyes and say, "Gracious Sophia, bless us with Your wisdom, fill us with Your peace, send us Your healing, and our prosperity increase."

Uncover your eyes, and cupping your hands over the flame, sweep the energy from the candles toward you three times. Then say, "Sacred Ruah, Blessed Flame, fill our home with Your Holy Name. Blessed Be." If a door or window is open, you may feel a slight breeze.

When you feel the Shekenah's presence, take out your prayer flags.

Using your markers, write your prayer on each flag. Try to correspond the request with the elemental color of the flag. For instance, if you wish to have better communication with a loved one, you might write that on a yellow square. Make sure there is enough room to make a slight fold over the cord after you are finished.

Glue or sew the flags on to the cord. If you have room on your altar, leave your flags on the table to dry and absorb the energy from the candles.

Open your circle, thanking the directions, angels and guides for their protection.

Ground your excess energy.

You can now enjoy the bread that evening and the next day, taking in its special energy. The candles can stay lit until you are going to bed, then be re-lit the next morning if you feel it is not safe to keep them burning during the night. Blow them out saying, "Breath of the Divine," or "Breath of

God." When you re-light them in the morning say, "Light of God (Divine)." Find a nice place out-side for your prayer flags and hang them up for the Sacred Ruah to take your prayers up to heaven. If you want to dedicate a change in your life or a life of a loved one, for example the beginning or end of menstruation, starting a new project, way of life, job or new path, change the last part of the prayer. Instead of "Fill our Home" say, "Bless this change in Your Holy Name." (Kelly, 2003.)

WISE WOMEN AND FOREMOTHERS

> …the old folk of Britain sometimes called upon "A pale wind and a purple wind,
> a black wind and a white…" to sweep away interference from their sacred place,
> protect it from harm and empower their spells.
>
> —Marian Green, *A Witch Alone*, 1995.

SAINT HILDEGARD

St. Hildegard of Bingen lived between 1098 and 1179. Benedictine abbess and mystic, she was called "the Sybil of the Rhine." She was born in Bockelheim, Germany. Sickly as a child, she was given to an aunt, Jutta, for care in a hermitage near Speyer. She founded Rupertsberg Convent near Bingen around 1147. She was one of the first great German mystics, a poetess and prophetess. Her music and poetry have remained popular over the centuries, all part of her recorded mystical experi-ences. Her best known work is *Scivias*, written between 1141 and 1151, relating twenty-six of her visions. Never formally canonized, Hildegard is regarded as a saint. The people of Bingen celebrate her feast day nonetheless. According to some sources, the paperwork was lost by the Vatican.

Music was extremely important to Hildegard. She describes it as the means of recapturing the original joy and beauty of paradise. Hildegard wrote hymns in honor of saints, virgins and Mary. She wrote in the plainchant tradition. Her music is undergoing a revival and enjoying huge public success. If you purchase some of Hildegard's works be sure to read the translations of the Latin text of the songs which provide a good example of Hildegard's writing. All her works are sung only by women.

Hildegard had visions of the Shekenah and would describe her visions to a scribe. Much of her herbal healing information came from her visions. Several herbalists and dentists have studied her works, and have found them to be quite sound. She often signed her letters to "stay moist and juicy." Hildegard is considered by some to be a wonderful herbalist and witch; Judith Berger points out that had she lived during a different time she would have been burned at the stake. (Berger, 1998.)

Here are some of Hildegard's beliefs:

- Our eyes are a mirror reflecting the mood of the soul. Bright eyes are signs of life. If someone is physically healthy, he or she has clear and sparkling eyes. Dull eyes are signs of death!
- Faulty metabolism may be caused by environmental stress and poor nutrition.
- Keep smiling.
- No other mental disturbance is as debilitating to a person as rage.

Hildegard's Feast day is September 17. I have called on St. Hildegard when I didn't know what herb to use and she has never failed me. There are times when I am stressed or in an emergency situation and have asked for her help; she always tells me what herbs to use and for how long.

RITUAL FOR HERBAL HEALING CRAFT

This is a ritual I created when I am making herbal tinctures, salves, or oils. I invoke Hildegard to my healing crafts. I also put out her picture and play her music when I am teaching herbal craft. You will need a green candle, a CD of Hildegard's music, a picture of the saint (optional) and the supplies for the herbal craft of your choice. If it is convenient and practical, create your sacred space before your prayer and work.

Prayer to St. Hildegard: "Holy Mother, bless me as I work with these herbs. Help me to heal using the green's power. Guide me as I create in my herbal craft. And bless me with your holy knowledge. So mote it be."

Create your tinctures, oils and salves, knowing that St. Hildegard watches and guides you. She will answer you with knowledge for healing if you call on her. When you are finished, open your circle, thanking Hildegard for her blessings.

BIDDY EARLY

O most powerful spirit of the bush with fragrant leaves, I am here again to seek wisdom. Give me tranquility and guidance to understand the mysteries of the forest and the knowledge of my ancestors.

—M. Rios in Müller-Ebeling, Rätsch and Storl, *Witchcraft Medicine*, 2003.

Ireland didn't have many witch burnings; most historians agree that they only burned four women for witchcraft. There is speculation that it was due to the healthy respect as well as the fear that the locals, including the clergy, had for wise women and cunning men. Others believe it is because these people went to church on Sunday even though on Monday they put out saucers of milk for the fey. Much of the congregation continued to practice the old ways while outwardly following the Catholic doctrines. (Robbins, 2004.)

Biddy Early was called the Wise Woman of Clare and her home was often crowded with people who benefitted from her wondrous cures. The Prince of Wales and the Queen of Gypsies were among her customers. As a traditional wise woman, Biddy never took money for her services; she was paid in whole pigs and whiskey. (Robbins, 2004.)

Her full name was Bridget Ellen Connors Early and she was born in 1798, the daughter of Ellen Early and John Thomas Connors. Following in her mother's footsteps as a healer, Biddy kept her mother's maiden name as her name. Outliving four husbands who died of drink, Biddy was considered a *cailleach*, an old wise woman who was an aspect of the ancient goddess. Biddy was described as having very red hair and a gold ring on every finger. (Robbins, 2004.)

Biddy had a magickal bottle that could see the past, present and future. It was said that it was a gift from the Sidhe (the fairies, pronounced *shee.)* Biddy lived with the fey for seven years and that was when she acquired the bottle, as well as knowledge of the healing arts and the use of herbs. She said that she could speak English, Irish and Sidhe. (Robbins, 2004.)

There were many stories about how Biddy got her bottle. Some say that her son, Tom, who died very young, brought it to her after he passed. Others say he won it at a game of hurling against the Sidhe. Still another story tells of Biddy baby-sitting a neighbor's child when the fairies stole the baby, replacing it with a changeling, which is a Sidhe child. The changeling became very fond of Biddy and he gave her the magickal bottle. (Robbins, 2004.) There is still much speculation as to how Biddy received her bottle, but because of it, peering into a bottle became a part of Irish folk craft. If a woman wants to divine for something, she makes a cylinder with her hands and peers into it for information. (McCoy, 1998.)

They say that if Biddy saw a coffin in her bottle, she sent the person away who had come for help, because there was nothing she could do. If she found the answer, she would send them away with a potion and instructions. Lady Gregory, a folklorist, traveled around the countryside in the late nineteenth and early twentieth centuries to collect stories of Biddy from the villagers who knew her. It was because of her miraculous cures that the priests were so against her and there were tales of the priests making it difficult for people to get in to see her. The priests took it as far as warning the locals against taking in any lodger who had traveled to see Biddy. (Robbins, 2004.)

There was a story of a priest who rode to Biddy's cottage to stop her from what she did. Apparently she stopped his horse in the middle of the road, and he could not make it move until he spit on it and said, "God bless you." They did try to put Biddy on trial for witchcraft in 1865, but the charges were dismissed because they could not find anyone to testify against her. Biddy died in 1874 with a priest at her side and a rosary around her neck. They say twenty-seven priests came to her funeral. There is speculation that the priests did this because they really didn't think she was so bad; I believe it is because they wanted to make sure she was dead. (Robbins, 2004.)

This past Beltaine the graduates of the Greenfire program, the Melissa, made a Biddy Bottle. The idea was researched by our Elder Darkstar. We had our choice of bottle and items to put it in. Darkstar cast a circle and we each created a bottle. We put herbs, crystals, essential oils, glitter, holy water made during a lunar eclipse, and rose water made at Litha. We were told to use our bottle at least three times a week and to expect not only to see things, but to hear them, too. Darkstar has suggested that for our future students we include the use of a Biddy Bottle from the beginning so that they can put things that represent their Wise Woman Studies in the bottle throughout the year, thus adding more power and meaning to their work. (Byrnes, 2009.)

Other famous wise women

Meg the Healer of Scotland was so good at being a healer that the fey came to her for help. It is said that Meg could walk freely between the world of Faery and the world of humans. She has been compared to a shaman in that she could walk between the worlds and bring back knowledge to help others. Some stories tell that she would find humans trapped in the world of the fey and would ask a local wizard to help free them. (McCoy, 1998.)

Mother Tarbat, a Scottish woman named Stine Bheag O'Tarbat, knew the secrets of weather magick. It is believed that this ability is given to crones and certain fairy folk. Biddy Mamionn of Innishark, Ireland, was a talented healer and midwife. They say that the fey took her in to help heal a child, and she exchanged healing lore with them. (McCoy, 1998.)

Pow-wow is a Pennsylvania Dutch healing system that is a blend of Native American lore with European folk craft. It is a combination of these arts combined with Bible verses. Those who practiced Pow-wow did not view themselves as witches, but Christians, and they were trained through oral tradition. The original Pow-wows were from Germany until the Scottish and Irish came around 1720. These people were similar to the Wise Woman and Cunning Man of other towns or villages in that people came to them for help. (Ravenwolf, 1999.)

Today we have other Wise Women in all areas of the United States and other countries. Some we know because they were wonderful enough to share their work. Each has their own specialty, but their focus is the same: to change the world and how things are done. Susun Weed writes books and teaches about herbal medicine. Julie de Bairacli Levy traveled throughout mostly Europe and the Middle East to learn about herbal medicine and natural healing, then wrote books about what she learned. Rosemary Gladstar also brings so much knowledge of natural healing and herbal craft to us through her publications. Judith Berger gave us a real treasure on herbal lore with her work.

From writers and Wise Women like Starhawk and Z. Budapest we learn about protecting the environment, women's rights and rituals. Diane Stein shares information with her research on alternative healing, crystals, chakras and meditations. Silver Ravenwolf, Ann Moura, Clarissa Pinkola-Estes, and Marion Green bring us their studies of ancient practices and traditions from different parts of the world. All of these women have shared their knowledge and experiences with us to help pave the way for the next group of women. They have molded my thought processes, changed the way I look at things and I bring their studies to my students to continue the cycle.

Notes—The Feminine Divine and Our Foremothers

Berger, J. *Herbal Rituals.* New York: St. Martin's Press, 1998.

Byrnes, C. personal communication, April 25, 2009.

Freedman, H. and Shachter, J. *Sanhedrin.* www.come-and-hear.com/sanhedrin/sanhedrin_0.html

Green, M. *A Witch Alone.* London: Thorsons, 1995.

Holy Bible Revised Standard Version: Book of Exodus. Chicago: International Council of Religious Education, 1928.

Kelly, P. *Saint Hildegard.* www.orderwhitemoon.org/goddess/StHilde.html, 2003.

Kelly, P. *Shekenah.* www.orderwhitemoon.org/goddess/Shekenah.html, 2003.

Labowitz, S. *God, Sex, and The Women of the Bible.* New York: Simon & Schuster, 1998.

Lewis, J. *Quote by Virginia Woolf.* www.womenshistory.about.com/library/qu/blqulist.htm, 2008.

Ravenwolf, S. *American Folk Magick: Charms, Spells and Herbals.* St. Paul: Llewellyn Publications, 1999.

Müller-Ebeling, C., Rätsch, C. and Storl, W. *Witchcraft Medicine: Healing Arts, Shamanic Practices and Forbidden Plants.* Rochester: Inner Traditions, 2003. (Rios, M.)

Robbins, T. *Wild Irish Roses: Tales of Brigits, Kathleens, and Warrior Queens.* York Beach: Conari Press, 2004.

Wisdom of Solomon. The New Oxford Annotated Bible, Augmented Third Edition, New Revised Standard Version, 2007. www.darshem.org/sys-tmpl/door/

Zsigmond, A. *"Mythology, Menstruation and the 'Woman with the Issue of Blood,'" The Goddess Within.* Issue 10, 42–44, 2009.

CHAPTER 10

BRINGING IT ALL TOGETHER

> *Before me, Raphael*
> *Behind me, Gabriel*
> *On my right is Michael*
> *On my left is Auriel*
> *Around me flames the Pentagram*
> *And above me shines the Six-Rayed Star*
> *Shekinah descend upon me now!*
>
> —Pow-wow prayer of protection,
> Silver Ravenwolf, *American Folk Magick*, 1999.

When a student comes to me to study I explain that we meet once a month for thirteen moons. Some women take longer because of busy lives, others finish right on time. There are many adjustments to their thinking and approach to the world when they delve into this. All of them come from different backgrounds, yet none of them get away from having their paradigms challenged. The graduate students, the Melissa, are always welcome to come back for the classes with the new students. This way they get to meet them. When they have finished their studies, they are welcomed into the Greenfire Clan. Since we are of different faiths and spiritual backgrounds as well as being solitary practitioners, we are more comfortable with the term *clan*. This makes our group not too tightly woven, but not too loose either. The Melissa meet semi-regularly throughout the year to celebrate the different Sabbats.

The first night we make an oil, a tincture and an infusion. We sit at the kitchen table and talk about how we got "here." Sometimes we sit in the garden, the sunroom or the living room. There is no ritual room. Always there are animals, cats and a dog; children are always welcome, because it would not be a folk craft without them. On this night I give them their Reiki I with the guidelines of what Reiki is and how to use it. They are sent away with the challenge to find an herbal ally to work with, get their books, write in their journal, Reiki themselves for 21 days, and find a form of the Feminine Divine.

The Greenfire Wise Woman reading list

Susun Weed (choose one of Susun's books):

> *Menopausal Years, The Wise Woman Way*
>
> *Healing Wise*
>
> *Wise Woman Herbal for the Childbearing Year*
>
> *Breast Cancer? Breast Health! The Wise Woman Way*

Diane Stein:

> *Essential Reiki: A Complete Guide to an Ancient Healing Art*

Judith Berger:

> *Herbal Rituals: Recipes for Everyday Living*

Z. Budapest (choose one of Z.'s books):

> *The Grandmother of Time: A Woman's Book of Celebrations, Spells, and Sacred Objects for Every Month of the Year*
>
> *Grandmother Moon: Lunar Magic in Our Lives—Spells, Rituals, Goddesses, Legends, and Emotions Under The Moon*

Clarissa Pinkola-Estes:

> *Women Who Run with the Wolves: Myths and Stories of the Wild Woman Archetype*

The next month I try to have a different herbal infusion ready for them. If the weather is nice we might take a weed walk in the garden. I try to do this when the weather is nice to let them experience herbal craft hands on. Many of my students never gardened, so the challenge for them to grow their herbs is even greater. We meet the elder tree in the garden and talk about folk tales connected to the plants as well as their healing powers. If they know their Reiki symbols and are comfortable, I give them their Reiki II. They are asked about how they are doing finding an ally and a Goddess. We talk about whether they have done Reiki on themselves, as well as whether they have written in their journal or purchased their books. I ask that they read the month they are in from Judith Berger's *Herbal Rituals* and from either of Z. Budapest's books, *Grandmother Moon* or *Grandmother Time*, the concept being that they understand the energy of each month that they are in. They should get the seeds or the plant of their herbal ally and start to sit by it, listening to it and using Reiki on it.

Each student's work is personal, and I do not teach each class exactly the same way. Some students come with an enormous amount of experience already and the classes are formed differently for them. There are some things I seem to follow regularly and one of those things is not moving on to other forms of energy healing until they have their Master/Teacher Reiki training. I try to get this to happen in their third or fourth month because they need to learn how to meld all the different modalities of healing. From there in the next months we work on chakras, then crystals and lastly aromatherapy. Each subject takes at least one month, although some students feel overwhelmed and wish to take two months on certain topics.

Throughout the time they study we discuss their work with their herbal ally, any other herbs they have chosen to work with, their journals, and the effect of the moon phase and the season on them. This is a very personal journey for each woman, and as they learn to heal others they are healing themselves. They always meet their demons, and those that finish the program have always dealt with them. The Greenfire women discuss the effect their change has on those closest to them and their reaction to their families or friends.

I have the students practice giving healings, attunements, making sacred space and running a ritual. The approaches are always different and eclectic because each woman has her own spiritual path. This gives them more confidence and experience.

HOLY WATER

This is an activity that I usually plan early on in the wise woman training. I like to do it near a Sabbat so it has the energies of that special time. The best time to make a batch of holy water is a lunar eclipse; the second best is the full moon. It is not necessary, but you can put your holy water under the full moon and make moon water to give it extra zing.

INGREDIENTS AND SUPPLIES:
- Jar(s)
- Spring water
- Sea salt
- Vervain
- Rose Water
- A drop of rum or vodka as a preservative.
- Sometimes we add lavender or lavender essential oil.

Cleanse your work area; smudging works well. Ground and center so you can focus on your intent to create this holy water. Take your container with the water in it, and call on your deity to charge it. At this point all of my students have their Reiki I or II so they usually Reiki it. When you are finished, put down the container and take your sea salt. Calling on your deity, add the salt three times. While doing this you can call on the Maid, Mother and Crone or Father, Son and Holy Spirit for instance, but you can also call on the deities and guides that you work with. Do the same for when you add the vervain.

Some people add seven drops of rose water, but because we usually work with Goddess energy, I have my students put in nine drops of rose water, as nine is a Goddess number. When you have added the rose water, hold the jar in your hands and charge it with Reiki. If you choose to use lavender essential oil you can put nine drops of this in; if you use lavender blossoms, follow the procedure used for the salt and vervain.

Make sure to charge the water after each ingredient. Then put about a teaspoon of vodka or rum in the water as a preservative, and you are finished. (Ravenwolf, 1999.)

Holy water can be used to cleanse and consecrate your sacred space, a person, your tools, or garden. Our clan elder, Darkstar, uses basil, which is considered a holy herb, whose folk name is Witch Grass, and sprinkles her holy water using the basil as her "sprinkler" wand. (Byrnes, 2008.)

LEVELS AND BELTS

Some wish to be part of covens, to share ceremonies and regular meetings with like-minded folk in the comfort of their own homes. Others, however, have heard wilder music playing to an older beat, and wish to reunite with Mother Nature, alone, out of doors, under the light of the stars and changing moonlight, in a simpler way... The solo occult path is a traditional one, following in the footsteps of the oracle, the hermit, the shaman or Druid priest.

—Marian Green, *A Witch Alone*, 1995.

True Wise Woman Craft has no need for initiations, levels, titles or belts. However, in this day and age people seem to need recognition for their work. There are four levels in Greenfire Wise Woman Craft, the first three occur about every four months, and the last occurs in the last month. The first level is Initiate, where the person is blessed in sacred space, as well as given a certificate and a white belt that is three yards long. The second level is Adept, and the person is given a certificate as well as a red belt the same length as the first. The third level is Wise Woman and Wisdom Keeper; the person is given a black belt. The last level is Melissa and is a green belt. Melissa is the title given to the priestesses that served Artemis and they are also the title of the bees that the serve the Queen bee in the hive.

The title of High Priestess implies more hierarchical thinking and behavior, which is not what this path should be about. The belts are colors in honor of the Maid, Mother, Crone, and Green Path. When each level is met, I discuss the energy of the Divine they are working with. Some women wear their belts around their waist during their sacred work; others hang them on their neck. They are usually kept by the altar and they are the sacred length of nine feet each. Sometimes people use the belts to mark off sacred space and put it around them during meditation or ritual work.

When the women have finished their studies, I give them my lineage of all the teachers I have studied with and who have initiated me so they can add their name on the bottom when they train others. This way they have a better understanding of who has influenced my teachings and know what energy has been passed on to them.

A RING, A ROBE AND A NAME

When a women is about to graduate from the Greenfire training, I suggest she dedicate a ring to wear as a symbol of her work. I wear a small white gold ring on my right hand that I never take off. It is my priestess ring that reminds me of who I am, what I have accomplished, and what path I have chosen to follow.

I also suggest that they get a robe for ceremonies; preferably green, because we are herbalists of the Greenfire clan. It is not necessary, but it is nice to have especially if she decides to visit other ceremonial circles. Lastly I suggest that the person consider a spiritual name. There are usually two names a women gets; one is a secret name only known to themselves and the Divine, and the other is a spiritual name one can share with others. Lately I have started to send the following letter to future graduates:

Dear —
For your initiation as a Melissa consider the following:

A ring
As a promise to yourself and the Goddess of what your path means to you. Consider it a wedding ring to yourself. The Goddess is in you, and you are marrying her. Ask yourself what this ring means to you. Where have you been? Where are you going? What does it mean to be Melissae?

A robe
A robe reminds you of the sacredness of your work and gives you warmth when meditating. It can provide protection as well as wrap you in sanctity.

A name
A name provides you with a connection to the Divine. You can do a vision quest to find your name. It is a reminder of the sacredness of your path.

With many Green and Bright Blessings ,
Amitofa Fox, Anam Cara
Greenfire Wise Woman Craft

I sign the letter with my title as *Anam Cara*. This is a Gaelic word for "Soul Friend" and since Wise Woman work is soul work, it makes sense to me to call myself this. "Mother" or "High Priestess" is too hierarchical and condescending to me. These women are my peers and friends; therefore they are my Soul Friends.

TRADITIONAL BLESSING
There are many variations of this blessing; I have found them in writings by Diane Stein and Silver Ravenwolf. Here is the version I use for each level and when my students feel they need some

comfort. I like to use this after each attunement also. I start at the person's feet, moving up as I continue the blessing.

GREENFIRE BLESSING

Feet	May you walk in truth, beauty, light and courage.
Knees	May you always remain humble and able to pray.
Root Chakra	May you always remain grounded and connected to the Mother Earth.
Sacral Chakra	May you always draw wisdom from your inner cauldron.
Solar Plexus	May you always have the energy to do what you need to do.
Heart Chakra	May you always be able to give and receive love as well as love yourself.
Throat chakra	May you always be able to speak with truth, beauty, clarity and compassion.
Third Eye	May you always be able to see the unseen.
Crown	May you always remain connected to the Divine.
	Blessed Be.

NOTES—BRINGING IT ALL TOGETHER

Byrnes, C. Personal communication, December 2008.

Green, M. *A Witch Alone.* London: Thorsons, 1995.

Ravenwolf, S. *American Folk Magick: Charms, Spells and Herbals.* St. Paul: Llewellyn Publications, 1999.

8289254R0

Made in the USA
Charleston, SC
25 May 2011